GO »
AHEAD

REALSCHULE BAYERN

8

Workbook

mit interaktiven Übungen

Deine **Audios** findest du auf scook.de/bayern. Dafür gibst du den unten stehenden Zugangscode in die Box ein.

Deine **interaktiven Übungen** kannst du so freischalten:

1. Melde dich auf scook.de/bayern an. Beim ersten Besuch von scook.de/bayern musst du dich mit einer – nicht notwendig personifizierten – E-Mailadresse registrieren.
2. Gib den unten stehenden Zugangscode in die Box ein.
3. Damit deine Lernstandsdaten gespeichert werden, müssen du und deine Eltern uns bei der ersten Freischaltung der interaktiven Übungen eine Einwilligung dazu geben. Cornelsen speichert die Antworten deiner durchgeführten Übungen für die Nutzungsdauer der interaktiven Übungen. Für Volljährige (über 18 Jahren) ist das Einverständnis der Eltern nicht erforderlich.

Die Nutzungsdauer für die Online-Übungen beträgt nach Aktivierung des Zugangscodes zwei Jahre. In dieser Zeit speichern wir deine Lernstandsdaten für dich; nach Ablauf der Nutzungsdauer werden sie gelöscht.

Dein Zugangscode auf **www.scook.de/bayern**

hkysg-yvnu4

Cornelsen

INHALT

So viele Zeichen im Workbook – was bedeuten sie?

Die Ampel – Wie schwer fällt dir eine Übung?
In der Ampel kannst du markieren, wie schwer dir eine (Teil-)Übung gefallen ist: rot = schwer, gelb = mittel, grün = leicht.

Weiße und blaue Kreise – jeder so gut er kann
Leichtere Aufgaben sind mit einem leeren Kreis markiert und schwierigere mit einem vollen. Die Übungen ohne spezielle Markierungen sind auf einem Niveau, das alle Schülerinnen und Schüler lösen können.

14

Kopfhörer – Hörtexte online
Für dieses Angebot lädst du dir auf scook.de/bayern alle Tonaufnahmen im MP3-Format herunter. Den Zugangscode dafür findest du auf S. 1 deines Workbooks. Die Zahl unter dem Kopfhörer nennt dir die Track-Nummer, unter der du den entsprechenden Hörtext hören kannst.

Das Tablet weist auf Online-Aufgabenpakete hin.
Gehe dazu auf scook.de/bayern, gib deinen Zugangscode von S. 1 ein und wähle aus dem Inhaltsverzeichnis die passende Übungszahl.

Stift, Partner- und Gruppenarbeit – wie du diese Übungen bearbeiten sollst
Für Aufgaben, neben denen ein Stift abgebildet ist, schreibst du deine Antwort auf ein anderes Blatt Papier. Die beiden Köpfe beziehen sich auf Übungen, die du zu zweit bearbeiten kannst. Die drei Köpfe auf Übungen, die du in einer Gruppe bearbeitest.

The American dream

Unit 1

Words and pictures

1 The American dream

a ⊙ Complete the definition with the correct words.

The American dream: a free, ____________ life which every American can ____________ through ____________ ____________.

easy hard reach relaxed achieve jobs a lot of happy work do

b Check your answer on SB page 11.

SB pp. 10–11

2 Personal histories

a Do you remember the teens from SB pp. 10–11? Match the information about their families (a–f and g–l) to the correct person (1–6).

name			His/Her family is ...	facts about teens and their families
1 Diego	☐	☐	a Mexican American.	g His/Her family owns a bank.
2 Zari	☐	☐	b German American.	h He/She wears a hijab.
3 Noor	☐	☐	c African American.	i His/Her great-granparents came to the US through Ellis Island.
4 Mattia	☐	☐	d Iranian American.	j His/Her grandparents came to the US with nothing but their clothes.
5 Ethan	☐	☐	e Vietnamese American.	k He/She became a citizen after ten years in the US.
6 Linh	☐	☐	f Italian American.	l His/Her family lives in Harlem.

01 b Listen to the teens and check your answers.

SB pp. 10–11

3 The Statue of Liberty

a What do the words on the Statue of Liberty mean? Tick (✓) the correct box.

SB pp. 10–11

- ☐ They invite people who have a hard life to come to the USA.
- ☐ They tell people that the air in the USA is very good.
- ☐ America only wants tired and poor people to come.

02 b Practise reading the words. Emphasize the important parts. Then listen to the poem to check your pronunciation.

New York City in song lyrics

1 *An open letter to NYC*

a Find two examples for each of the categories (1–5) in the song lyrics *An open letter to NYC* (below). Use words from the box. There are four words you don't need.

Asian • Battery • blends • Bronx • cars • dedicates • prize fighters • Queens • skyscrapers • subway • tests • trees • white • writers

1 boroughs of NYC	Brooklyn	______	______
2 tall things in NYC	brownstones	______	______
3 races or ethnic groups in NYC	Middle Eastern	______	______
4 jobs of New Yorkers	Wall Street traders	______	______
5 things that NYC does	mends	______	______

b What is each part of the song about? Write the correct letter in each box. One definition is missing. Fill in what you think this part is about.

1 Brooklyn, Bronx, Queens and Staten From the Battery to the top of Manhattan Asian, Middle Eastern and Latin Black, white, New York you make it happen	☐	a Saying thank you to the city for bringing people together
2 Brownstones, water towers, trees, skyscrapers Writers, prize fighters and Wall Street traders We come together on the subway cars Diversity unified, whoever you are	☐	b NYC has stayed strong after the attacks
3 Dear New York, this is a love letter To you and how you brought us together We can't say enough about all you do 'Cause in the city we're ourselves and electric too	☐	c Boroughs and races/ ethnic groups in NYC
4 I see you're still strong after all that's gone on Lifelong, we dedicate this song Just a little something to show some respect To the city that blends and mends and tests	☐	d Life in NYC still goes on after the attacks on the World Trade Center
5 Since 9/11 we're still livin' And lovin' life we've been given Ain't nothing gonna take that away from us We're lookin' pretty and gritty 'cause in the city we trust	☐	e ______
6 Dear New York, I know a lot has changed Two towers down but you're still in the game Home to the many, rejecting no one Accepting peoples of all places, wherever they're from	☐	f Different sights and people in the city

SB pp. 12–13

2 Facts about 9/11 and the WTC

a Are these statements about 9/11 and the WTC true or false? Tick (✓) the correct boxes.

	true	false
1 WTC stands for World Tourist Center.	☐	☐
2 9/11 is how Americans write 11 September.	☐	☐
3 The old WTC had three towers.	☐	☐
4 The new One WTC is also called the Freedom Tower.	☐	☐
5 The holes from the old WTC are still empty.	☐	☐

b Correct the false statements.

____

____

____

SB pp. 12–13

3 More songs about New York City

a Change the order of the letters to find a nickname for NYC from the song by Alicia Keys (SB p. 13).

P	E	I	M	E	R		T	A	S	E	T

b The line "If I can make it here, I can make it anywhere" of the song is borrowed from another famous song about NYC. Use the internet to find the name and artist of the song.

Name: ____________________ Artist: ____________________

c What other songs about NYC do you know or can you find (online / on CDs / ...)? Choose one and make notes on the following questions. Then present it in class. You can also present the song from b.

- What is the title and who is the artist of the song?
- What is the style of the song? (rock/rap/classical/pop/jazz/...)
- What is the song about? (subject of the song / message of the song)
- What is your favourite line of the song?

SB pp. 12–13

Our dreams

1 Life in a homeless shelter

a A new family in Diego's shelter has questions about the rules. Match the questions and answers.

1 When can we check into the shelter? ☐
2 Can we bring our dog with us? ☐
3 How many bags may we bring? ☐
4 Are there babysitters for children at the shelter? ☐
5 Is alcohol allowed in the shelter? ☐
6 Are there rules about keeping the rooms clean? ☐

a Each person may only bring two large bags or three small bags.
b Yes, you can ask for a babysitter.
c No, pets are not allowed in the shelter.
d You may check into the shelter between 5 and 8 pm.
e No, drinking is not allowed in the building.
f Yes, rooms must be cleaned every day.

b Fill in the missing words to make four more questions about the shelter.

1 ________ (modal verb) we have visitors?
2 ________ (question word) many people live in the shelter?
3 ________ (auxiliary verb) there roaches here?
4 ________ (question word) is the curfew?

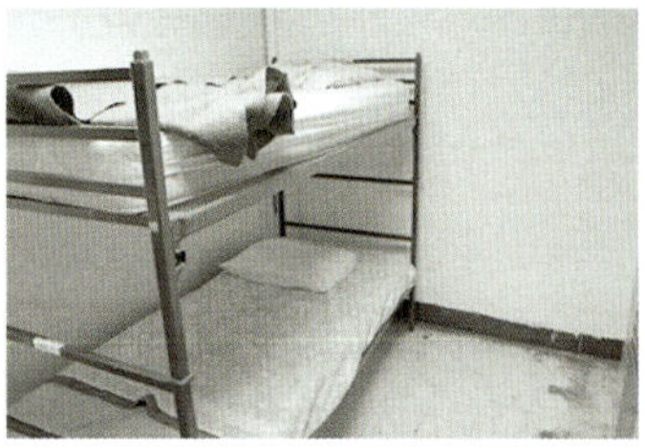

SB pp. 14–15

2 An interview with Diego

a Put the words in the right order to make questions.

1 is / how / Diego / old /?
____
2 Diego's father / did / health insurance / have /?
____
3 the rent / why / Diego's mother / afford / couldn't /?
____
4 would / what job / to do / Diego / like /?
____

03 b Answer the questions. Then listen to the interview with Diego and check your answers. SB pp. 14–15

1 ________________________________
2 ________________________________
3 ________________________________
4 ________________________________

A form

1 Travel application for the USA

Complete the text about applying to travel to the USA. Use the words in the box.

applicant • application • citizenship • enter • expiration • fill in • harm • issue • property

To visit the USA, you need to ____________ an ____________ form. You must ____________ basic information about yourself, like your name, date of birth and address. You also need to tell them your country of ____________ : that may not be the country where you were born! They ask for your passport number as well as the ____________ and ____________ dates: they want to know when you got your passport and when you need a new one. Each ____________ also has to answer some very personal questions, for example if you've ever committed a crime that resulted in serious ____________ to ____________ or another person.

SB p. 16

2 The form

04

Caden and his father are planning a trip to the USA. Listen to them and fill in the form.

SB p. 16

ENTER INFORMATION Please give all answers in English.
Required fields are shown by a red asterisk*.

APPLICANT / PASSPORT INFORMATION
Refer to your passport and enter all information in the same format.

Family Name* ____ First Name* ____

Gender* ○ Male ○ Female

Date of Birth* ____ City of Birth* ____

Country of Birth* ____ Passport Number* ____

Country of Citizenship* ____ National Identification Number ____

Issue Date* ____ Issuing Country* ____

Personal Identification Number ____ Expiration Date* ____

YOUR CONTACT INFORMATION
Please enter your contact information below.

Address Line 1* ____

Address Line 2 ____

Apartment Number ____ City* ____

State/Province/Region* ____ Country* ____

Telephone Type* ____ Country Code + Phone* ____

Email Address* ____

SOCIAL MEDIA (Optional)
Please enter information about your online activity.

Provider / Platform ____

Social Media Identity ____

CONTACT INFORMATION WHILE IN THE U.S.

Name* ____

Address Line 1* ____

Address Line 2 ____

Apartment Number ____

City* ____

State* ____

Phone* Number ____

EMERGENCY CONTACT INFORMATION IN OR OUT OF THE U.S.
(family member or friend)

Family Name* ____ First (Given) Name* ____

Email Address* ____ Telephone* ____

QUESTIONS

1 Do you have a physical or mental illness?* ____
Are you a drug user or addict?* ____
Do you have a disease?* ____

2 Have you ever committed a crime that resulted in serious harm to property or another person?* ____

Source: U. S. Department of Homeland Security

Visiting the USA

05 1 LISTENING At a New York hotel

Fiona and Fred are getting ready to check out of their hotel in New York. Listen to their conversation and fill in the form. Tick ☺ or ☹ for each question. SB p. 17

MIDNIGHT MANHATTAN HOTEL FEEDBACK FORM

		☺	☹
1	Were you happy with the size of your room?	☐	☐
2	Was the price of your room fair?	☐	☐
3	Was the room comfortable?	☐	☐
4	Was everything clean?	☐	☐
5	Was the wardrobe big enough?	☐	☐
6	Did the room have a good view?	☐	☐
7	Was the room quiet?	☐	☐

Your room number: ______

2 MEDIATION Travelling around New York

You're at a hotel in NYC with your grandfather. You want to ask the receptionist how to get from your hotel to the World Trade Center. Help your grandfather with the conversation. SB p. 17

Grandfather: *Sag ihm, wir möchten zum World Trade Center. Wie kommen wir hin?*

You: 1 ______?

Receptionist: You can take a bus, the subway or a taxi.

You: 2 ______.

Grandfather: *Ein Taxi klingt gut. Frag ihn bitte, wie lange das dauert.*

You: 3 ______?

Receptionist: About 25 minutes.

You: 4 ______.

Grandfather: *Und was kostet das?*

You: 5 ______?

Receptionist: I'm not sure. Probably about 30 dollars.

You: 6 ______.

Grandfather: *Was gibt man einem Taxifahrer für ein Trinkgeld in den USA?*

You: 7 ______?

Receptionist: Usually about 15–20 % of the fare.

You: 8 ______.

Grandfather: *Oh, das ist viel! Frag ihn bitte, wo wir ein Taxi finden.*

You: 9 ______?

Receptionist: There are usually a few right in front of the hotel.

You: 10 ______.

Big Apple Greeters

1 All about the Greeters

a Below are some questions about a group called Big Apple Greeters. Cross out the wrong form of each questions.

	a	b
1	What does a Big Apple Greeter do?	What does a Big Apple Greeter?
2	Where take Big Apple Greeters visitors?	Where do Big Apple Greeters take visitors?
3	Who started Big Apple Greeters?	Who did Big Apple Greeters start?
4	How much does it cost to meet a Big Apple Greeter?	How much costs it to meet a Big Apple Greeter?
5	What like tourists about the Greeters?	What do tourist like about the Greeters?
6	Who do I contact to plan a tour?	Who contact I to plan a tour?

b Decide if the correct questions from a are subject questions or object questions. Write *s* or *o*. You can look at SB p. 18 for help.

1	2	3	4	5	6

c Match each of the answers below with the correct question from a.

a To more than 100 neighbourhoods around the city. [2]

b It's free! [ ]

c Fill in the form on our website to contact Big Apple Greeters. [ ]

d That they are friendly volunteers who show them their NYC. [ ]

e The Greeter shows visitors part of life in New York City. [ ]

f A New Yorker named Lynn Brooks. [ ]

SB pp. 18–19

2 Film tour of New York City

Your friend has found a tour group that goes to places where famous films were made. He phones them to ask for more information. Write the questions with the words below.

1 who – lead – tour ______________________

2 where – we – go – on the tour ______________________

3 when – tour – start ______________________

4 how many people – in – be – tour group ______________________

5 cost – how much – it ______________________

6 we – visit – the deli – from *Enchanted* ______________________

SB pp. 18–19

3 Gracie Mansion

Your Greeter is showing you Gracie Mansion. Complete the questions.

1 What ______________ The name of this building is Gracie Mansion.
2 Who ______________ Gracie Mansion belongs to the city.
3 ________ lives here? The mayor[1] of New York lives there.
4 Who ______________ Archibald Gracie, who built the mansion, gave it his name.
5 How many bedrooms ______________ It has five bedrooms.
6 ________ may sleep here? Only the mayor's family and official visitors may sleep here.
7 ______________ mayors have lived here? Ten mayors have lived in it.

SB pp. 18–19

[1] **mayor** Bürgermeister/in

4 British and American English

You and your friend are in NYC, but Simon can't remember the words for these things in American English. Write the words on the lines.

____

____

____

____

____

____

SB pp. 12–23

Using what you know

1 Explaining what you want

a Circle the correct word in each phrase.

1 It's a long thing *who / what / that* helps you put on your shoes.
2 I *use / buy / need* something for swimming, to see under the water.
3 I also want a *couple / type / set* of shoes. You wear them in the summer.
4 You *wear / use / want* it to put your clothes in when you go on a trip.
5 I only brought T-shirts on this trip. I need *anything / something / more*, so I don't get cold.

b What things are they describing in a? Use the words from the box. There are three words you don't need.

1 ______________ 4 ______________
2 ______________ 5 ______________
3 ______________

backpack • boots • bracelet • goggles • jacket • sandals • shoehorn • swimsuit

c Now listen and check your answers. 06 SB p. 20

2 SPEAKING Around New York

a Partner B: Look at page 71. Partner A: You and your partner are tourists in New York. You want to go sightseeing, but can't remember the names of these places. Describe them to your partner. For example: It is a place where ... / You can do/see ... there.

b Now change roles. Which of the following places is Partner B describing? Tick (✓) the correct sights and tell her/him the name of each place. SB p. 20

☐ World Trade Center / Freedom Tower

☐ Bronx Zoo

☐ Statue of Liberty

☐ Brooklyn Bridge

☐ Central Park

Putting Makeup on the Fat Boy

1 Carlos' big day

a **Answer the questions about Carlos' big day (SB pp. 22–23). You don't have to write complete sentences.**

1 WHAT is the important event on Carlos' big day? ______

2 WHEN does it happen? ______

3 WHERE does it happen? ______

4 WHO is it with? ______

5 WHY does Carlos go to the men's room in Macy's? ______

b **Find the lines in the story with the information below. Write the line numbers.**

1 The manager of FeatureFace Cosmetics acts like he's very important. ______

2 The manager has a lot to do on Saturday. ______

3 Carlos made his nails look good for the interview. ______

4 Rosalia doesn't come to their meeting place. ______

5 A person who works at the store gives Carlos a strange look. ______

6 Carlos feels good in his boots. ______

7 Carlos doesn't want to go to the interview without Rosalia. ______

8 Carlos doesn't like Rosalia's outfit. ______

c **What do you think happened at the interview? Write Carlos' diary entry about the interview.**

SB pp. 22–23

1 Check your vocabulary

a Complete the text about visiting New York.

There are a lot of ways to get around the five ______________ of New York. For example, you can take one of 27 subway ______________ or hail a ______________. There's usually a lot of ______________ in New York, so taxis can be quite slow! When you arrive, the driver will tell you the ______________. Give a ______________ of about 15–20 %.
If you're staying at a hotel, you will check ______________ with the receptionist. Make sure to get a ______________ card for each person in your room. Don't forget: what Americans call the ______________ floor is the ground floor in the UK.

b Match the words in the two boxes. Write the words and phrases on the lines.

vending	an application
state of	date
homeless	insurance
health	machine
fill in	mind
expiration	shelter

1 ______________
2 ______________
3 ______________
4 ______________
5 ______________
6 ______________

2 Check your language

You meet a friendly tourist at your hotel. Ask her questions about herself.

1 ______________ I'm from Rome, Italy.
2 ______________ Yes, it's my first time in New York.
3 ______________ I'm staying for one week.
4 ______________ Because I wanted to visit the places I have seen in movies.
5 ______________ Yes, I think New York is amazing!
6 ______________ I'm in room 891.
7 ______________ Oh, that's my mother.
8 ______________ We're going to the Empire State Building this morning and to the American Museum of Natural History in the afternoon.

3 Check your listening and speaking

07

a Zara and Jordan are checking in at a hotel in NYC. Listen to their conversation and compare it with the text below. Underline the eight words/phrases that are different. Then listen again and write them down on the right.

Receptionist:	Welcome to the Midnight Manhattan Hotel. How can I help you?	______
Zara:	Yes, please. We've booked a room for three nights.	______
Receptionist:	What's the name of the person who booked the room?	______
Zara:	Zara Elliott. That's me.	______
Receptionist:	Ah, yes, Ms Elliot. So here's your key card. It's room 318 on the 3rd floor.	______
Jordan:	Can we have two key cards?	______
Receptionist:	No problem. Here you are.	______
Zara:	Where's the elevator?	______
Receptionist:	It's over there, on the right.	______
Jordan:	Oh, I see it. Thank you.	______
Zara:	When is checkout?	______
Receptionist:	You have to leave the room by 11:00 am.	______
Jordan:	OK, thank you.	______

b Practise the conversation with two partners.

4 Check your writing

Fill in the missing words on this form.

__________ Information

Name: *Zara* *Elliott* ____ of Birth: *5/19/2000*

_____ Name ______ Name Gender: ◎ ____ ◎ ______

Are you a _______ of the United States? ◎ YES ◎ NO

If not, _______ of citizenship? *England*

Passport Number? *09829571093*

_____ Date: *3/4/2020* ___________ Date: *3/4/2030*

Talking together

1 How are we the same?

a **Preparing to speak: Write answers to the following questions in complete sentences.**

1 In what month is your birthday? ______________________.

2 How do you get to school? ______________________.

3 How many brothers and sisters do you have? ______________________.

4 Where did you go on your last holiday? ______________________.

5 Have you ever been to England? If so, when? ______________________

______________________.

6 What are your plans for this afternoon? ______________________.

7 What did you have for breakfast this morning? ______________________.

8 What book are you reading at the moment? ______________________.

9 What's your favourite sport? ______________________.

b **Speaking: Ask your partner the questions and compare your answers. Find three answers that are the same. You can also ask more questions to find out things that are the same.**

c **Presenting: Tell the class what's the same about you and your partner.**

To practise describing pictures, look at page 29, exercise 1.

2 In New York City

a **Look at the photos on page 16. Take turns describing one of the photos (Partner A: Statue of Liberty, Partner B: Central Park). Your partner has to find out which one it is.**

b **You are going to prepare a two-minute dialogue. You and your partner are in New York City. Partner A wants to visit the Statue of Liberty. Partner B wants to go to Central Park. Your parents say that you have to stay together.**

- Think about why you want to go to the Statue of Liberty / Central Park. What do you want to do there? What do you like about it?
- Why don't you want to do the other activity? What are the disadvantages?
- Look at the pictures on the next page to get some ideas.
- Take three minutes to prepare. Make notes on the next page. Write down your reasons.

Helpful phrases

- I'd like to go to ... because ...
- I think/feel/believe that ...
- In my opinion, ...
- If you ask me, ...
- I don't think it's a good idea to ... because ...
- You've got a good point there, but ...
- I don't agree with you about ...
- I am not sure that ...

My notes: ______________________________

____

____

____

____

____

____

c Talk to your partner. Decide together where to go and why.

Land of the free?

Unit 2

Words and pictures

1 Grace's presentation

08

a Listen to Grace from SB p. 27. What aspects of life in the pueblo does Grace talk about in her presentation? Tick (✓) the right boxes.

1 traditional clothes	☐	5 languages	☐
2 transport	☐	6 family	☐
3 schools	☐	7 sports	☐
4 government	☐	8 crime	☐

b Fill in the missing words, using information from Grace's presentation.

1 Kewa	Grace is a ________ of this ________ .
2 adobe	Grace lives in this kind of house on a ________ .
3 stereotype	One of these is that ________ ________ have only one culture.
4 indigenous people	They lived in America before ________ people settled there.
5 casinos	Some reservations make a lot of ________ with these.
6 braids	Grace wears her ________ in these.
7 headdress	You have to earn the ________ to wear one of these.

08

c Listen again and check your answers in a and b.

SB pp. 26–27

2 Word game

a Write the words under the pictures.

________ ________ ________ ________ ________ house

b Add or change letters to the words below to spell three of the words from a.

1 father: add one letter
2 read: change one letter
3 bread: change two letters

________ ________ ________

SB pp. 26–27

Trail of Tears

1 The story *Trail of Tears*

a **How do you say goodbye to a place you love? Write down three ideas. Share with a partner.**

____

____

____

b **Put the events of the story *Trail of Tears* (SB pp. 28–29) in the right order (1–11).**

- **a** A baby girl died on the journey. ☐
- **b** Many people who took the blankets died. ☐
- **c** Soldiers burnt the family's house. ☐
- **d** A mother and her son watched people saying goodbye to their home. 1
- **e** The boy took his mother's body into the woods. ☐
- **f** The boy saw his mother's spirit in the night for the first time. ☐
- **g** The family started walking to a new home with many other people. ☐
- **h** Soldiers gave blankets to the Choctaw, but the boy's mother didn't take them. ☐
- **i** The boy's father found the mother dead in the morning. ☐
- **j** The family carried the mother's bones to their new home. ☐
- **k** The mother's spirit came to her son a second time. ☐

c **Why did these things happen? Match the events (1–8) and their reasons (a–h).**

1. People rubbed their backs on trees and crawled on the river stones to ☐
2. The boy and his family were cold because ☐
3. People took blankets from the soldiers because ☐
4. The Native Americans walked to ☐
5. A mother carried her dead daughter because ☐
6. The spirit of the boy's mother came to him for the first time because ☐
7. The *shilombish* came to the boy for the second time to ☐
8. The mother's spirit wanted her body to be bones so that ☐

- **a** their house had burnt and they didn't have anything to wear.
- **b** a new home that the whites couldn't take away from them.
- **c** she wanted to bury her near her new home.
- **d** she had died.
- **e** say goodbye to their home.
- **f** it would be easier for her family to carry.
- **g** show him where to carry his mother's body.
- **h** they were cold.

SB pp. 28–29

2 Words from the story

a What are these things? Write the words under the pictures.

b Find verbs in *Trail of Tears* from the same word families. Write the infinitive forms below.

	Noun	Adjective	Verb
1	rub		*to*
2	pull		
3	blood	bloody	
4	crawl		
5	infection	infectious	
6	beginning	beginning	
7	burial	buried	
8	lift		
9	float; floatation	floaty	

c Put the words and phrases from the story in the correct categories.

~~awake~~ • blood • bones • bury • knee • make your way to • mud • river • road • spirit • swamp • wagon

1 body *awake*

2 nature

3 travel

4 death

SB pp. 28–29

Time for change

1 Problems at the pueblo

Find the right clause to end each type 0 *if*-sentence. Make sure to use the right forms of the verbs.

Use type 0 *if*-sentences to talk about facts.

SB pp. 30–31

(not have) health insurance • *(drop out)* of school • *(not go)* to the doctor • *(be)* unemployed

It's hard to ...

1 get a job if you ______________________.

2 get health insurance if you ______________________.

3 pay for doctors if you ______________________.

4 stay healthy if you ______________________.

2 At the pueblo school

a Read what the kids in Grace's class are saying. Match the clauses to make type 1 *if*-sentences.

Use type 1 *if*-sentences to talk about future results.

1 If John is hungry this afternoon, ☐ | a if I need more facts for my report.
2 I'll do online research ☐ | b you'll go on trips for games.
3 If I get good grades, ☐ | c if she makes some friends.
4 Anna will like school more ☐ | d if the bus doesn't come on time.
5 If you join the basketball team, ☐ | e he'll eat in the cafeteria.
6 They'll be late for school tomorrow morning ☐ | f I'll go to college.

b Highlight the commas in the sentences from a. When is there a comma in an *if*-sentence?

____

SB pp. 30–31

3 What would happen if ...?

Fill in the gaps to make type 2 *if*-sentences.

Use type 2 *if*-sentences to talk about unlikely situations.

1 If I *had* (have) a million dollars, I __________ __________ (buy) new smartphones for all my friends.

2 If he __________ (be) president, he *would ban* (ban) guns.

3 If there __________ (be) no more diseases, people __________ (live) longer.

4 If I __________ (live) in the US, my English __________ (be) better.

SB pp. 30–31

Talking about a film

1 Spirit Game: Pride[1] of a Nation

a MEDIATION You and your friend are writing a report about the Native American Iroquois tribe. You think the film *Spirit Game: Pride of a Nation* might help you. Your friend has some questions about the film. Answer them in German, using information from the review.

Lacrosse was invented[2] by the Native American Haudenosaunee tribe more than 1,000 years ago. In 2015, the World Lacrosse Championships took place in Onondaga, New York, homeland[3] of the Haudenosaunee (who were called the Iroquois by the French). The documentary film 'Spirit Game: Pride of a Nation' tells the story of the Iroquois Nationals lacrosse team's road to the championships.

This event was important because it was the first time that an international sports competition was held on a reservation. The film also tells how much the game means to the Haudenosaunee: they call it their medicine game and believe that it can help the body and spirit. The championships gave the Iroquois as a nation the chance to play their own game on their own land, to show their flag, share their culture, and welcome guests from around the world.

Through interviews with experts, the film gives a lot of information about the history of the Haudenosaunee and the game of lacrosse. We also learn about the difficulties that the Iroquois Nationals faced: in 2010, for example, England would not let the team into the country to compete[4] in the world championships because the government wouldn't accept the nation's passports.

In 'Spirit Game' of course you can also see a lot of film material from the 2015 championship games. Although it's exciting to watch, there may be too much of it for people who aren't big lacrosse fans. It's also hard to figure out the focus of the film. Is it about the history of lacrosse? The Iroquois team's fight to play in and hold the championships? Is it about the 2015 championship? The fight of the Haudenosaunee to be seen as a nation?

It doesn't really matter[5]: 'Spirit Game' is a very interesting film with information about all of these topics. The stars of the film are the four Thompson brothers, professional players who competed on the Iroquois Nationals team in the championships. It was the first time they had played together since they were children and very exciting for them and the team's fans ... and scary for the other teams!

Anyone interested in sports and Native American history or culture should watch this film.

[1] **pride** Stolz [2] **invent** erfinden [3] **homeland** Heimat [4] **compete** im Wettkampf antreten [5] **matter** wichtig sein

1 Worum geht es in dem Film? ______________________________

____

2 Warum waren diese Spiele so wichtig für die Iroquois? ______________________________

____

____

3 Warum haben die Iroquois Nationals an der Weltmeisterschaft 2010 nicht teilgenommen?

____

4 Was wurde am Film kritisiert? ______________________________

____

5 Wer sind die Thompson-Brüder? ______________________________

____

b SPEAKING Would you like to watch the film? Why (not)? Discuss with a partner. SB p. 33

Do guns make us free?

1 Opinions about guns

a **How do these Americans feel about guns? Circle the correct word(s) in each quote.**

	1 How should my daughter protect *herself / himself* without a gun?
	2 I don't own a gun. I would worry about my son accidentally hurting or killing *hisself / himself* with it.
	3 When people shoot *each other / ourselves,* it only creates more problems: only police officers should have guns.
	4 We own guns, so we can protect *ourselves / each other*.
	5 I'm afraid when I am by *myself / yourself*, so I want to buy a gun.
	6 The police aren't always there to help you: you need to be able to help *themselves / yourself* if there's trouble.

b **Jose and Nevaeh are talking about yesterday's debate. Complete their dialogue with *each other* or a reflexive pronoun (*myself, himself, herself,* etc.).**

Jose: You did really well in the debate yesterday. How did you prepare for it?

Nevaeh: Well, I practised a little at home and watched ________________ in the mirror sometimes. Ms Evans recommended that we make videos of ________________, so I did that too.

Jose: I could tell you had practised: you really expressed ________________ clearly.

Nevaeh: Thank you! I also informed ________________ about gun control and gun rights as much as possible. I read three articles on the topic!

Jose: You really seemed to know a lot about it. Much more than the guy you were debating with! And you were much friendlier.

Nevaeh: I think it's really important to respect ________________ and listen to ________________ in a debate. And I try not to take ________________ too seriously: debating should be fun!

SB pp. 34-35

2 Gun control and gun rights slogans

a Read the slogans from the gun control and gun rights movements. Match each one to the right movement.

1 You can have my gun when you take it from my cold, dead hands.

2 *Protect children, not guns.*

3 Not one step back.

4 Our blood. Your hands.

5 Guns don't kill people; people kill people.

6 *More guns, less crime.*

7 ENOUGH.

8 No more silence[2]. End gun violence.

9 *I carry a gun because a cop[1] is too heavy.*

10 Violence is the problem, not the solution.

[1] cop *(infml)* Polizist/in
[2] silence Schweigen

b Choose your favourite slogan. Is it from the gun rights movement or the gun control movement? Complete the sentences.

I picked the slogan ______________________________.

It means ______________________________

______________________________.

I know it's from the ______________ movement because ______________

______________________________.

I like it because ______________________________

______________________________.

SB pp. 34–35

3 A debate about guns

09

Listen to the beginning of a debate. Fill in the gaps with information from the text.

1 The topic of the debate is: gun control ______________.

2 Always Right says that ______________ make places ______________.

3 They also think that fewer guns make it harder to ______________ other people and to commit ______________.

4 Their third argument is that stricter ______________ would make it harder to ______________ at stores.

SB pp. 34–35

Doing online research

1 Online research on a Native American tribe

a Morgan has to give a presentation on a Native American tribe for her history class. Put the steps for her online research in the right order (1–6).

- [ ] Look carefully at the search engine results.
- [ ] Make notes on key information.
- [ ] Refer to sources on slides, poster, etc.
- [ ] Research the topic.
- [ ] Write down text sources.
- [ ] Choose a topic.

b Morgan has chosen the topic "The Mashantucket Pequot tribe in Connecticut" for her presentation. When she searches for information, she finds the following webpages. Tick (✓) if she should use each webpage as a source and explain your choice. You don't have to write complete sentences. Think about the topic of Morgan's presentation and the class it is for.

Website	Use?		Why (not)?
	Yes	No	
a Mashantucket Pequot Museum and Research Center webpage (.org)	☐	☐	
b The Mashantucket Pequot Tribal Nation webpage (.gov)	☐	☐	
c Mashantucket Pequot travel guide	☐	☐	
d The New York Times: news story	☐	☐	
e Jobs with the Mashantucket Pequot	☐	☐	

c Highlight the following information on a webpage from the Pequots.

1 Size of the tribe and its land at different times
2 First war with the colonists
3 Result of war for the Pequots
4 When and why members came back

Tribal History

The history of the Mashantucket Pequot Tribal Nation is one of dramatically changing fortunes. Native peoples have continuously occupied Mashantucket in Southeastern Connecticut for over 10,000 years. By the early 17th century, just prior to European contact, the Pequots had approximately 8,000 members and inhabited 250 square miles. However, the Pequot War (1636–1638) – the first major conflict between colonists and an indigenous New England people – had a devastating impact on the Tribe.
When the Pequot War formally ended, many tribal members had been killed and others placed in slavery or under the control of other tribes. Those placed under the rule of the Mohegans eventually became known as the Mashantucket (Western) Pequots […].
In the ensuing decades, the Pequots battled to keep their land, while at the same time losing reservation members to outside forces. By 1774, a Colonial census indicated that there were 151 tribal members in residence at Mashantucket. By the early 1800s, there were between 30 and 40 […], by 1856 illegal land sales had reduced the 989-acre reservation to 213 acres.
In the early 1970s, tribal members began moving back to the Mashantucket reservation, hoping to restore their land base and community, develop economic self-sufficiency, and revitalize tribal culture. ◇

d Do online research about the tribal symbol of the Mashantucket Pequots and make notes. Describe the symbol and explain its meaning. Write down your source(s).

SB p. 36

A profile of a protester

1 The Parkland shooting

Fill in the gaps with information from the text on SB p. 38.

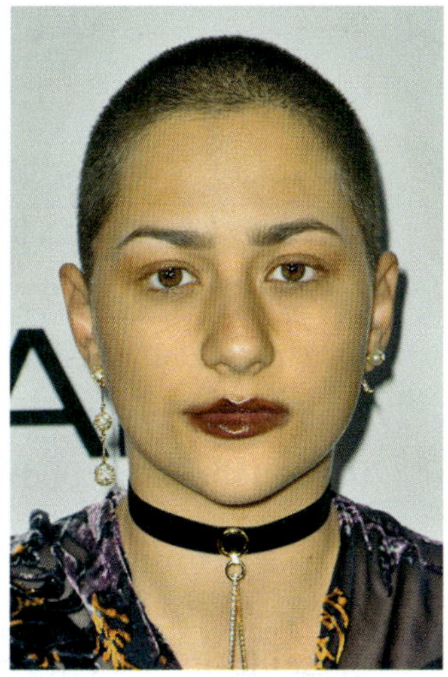

On ____________ 14, 2018 there was a mass ____________ at the Marjory Stoneman Douglas School in Parkland, ____________. A ____________ killed ____________ teachers and students in ____________ minutes and twenty-two seconds. Emma González ____________ the shooting and now fights for stricter ____________ ____________ laws.

SB pp. 38-39

2 Emma González

Use the profile of Emma González on SB pp. 38–39 to fill in the information about her.

a President of: ____________

b Hair: ____________

c Worst experience: ____________

d Protests for: ____________

e Nationality on father's side: ____________

f Two events where she has given speeches: 1. ____________ 2. ____________

g Face of this movement: ____________

SB pp. 38-39

3 Protest methods

Which of the following methods of protesting are referred to in the profile? Tick (✔) the four boxes.

- ☐ a making a computer presentation
- ☐ b wearing a T-shirt
- ☐ c taking part in a march
- ☐ d creating a webpage
- ☐ e social media
- ☐ f writing letters
- ☐ g speaking with politicians
- ☐ h giving a speech

SB pp. 38-39

4 Gun control laws

a Paragraph 3 on SB p. 38 describes three changes to gun control laws that Emma González wanted. What are they?

1 ____________________

2 ____________________

3 ____________________

b "In March 2018 the state of Florida introduced stricter gun control laws" (lines 50–52). Read about the new laws below. Which two laws do what Emma González wanted? Tick (✔) the correct boxes. Explain why.

☐ 1 Minimum age to buy a gun increased from 18 to 21

☐ 2 More money to make schools safer

☐ 3 Ban on "bump stocks" (equipment to make normal guns shoot faster)

☐ 4 Let some people who work in schools carry guns

☐ 5 New three-day wait to buy a gun

____

SB pp. 38-39

5 Opposites

Find words with the opposite meanings in the text. The paragraph numbers will help you.

1 to let (hair) grow (1)	____________	4 crime (3)	____________
2 gay (1)	____________	5 silence (4)	____________
3 to die (2)	____________	6 real (5)	____________

SB pp. 38-39

6 Crossword puzzle

ACROSS
2 without sound
4 a feeling of being embarrassed or sad
7 sth. that you have done or that happens to you
8 to have sth. as part of a group or total
9 to give help to sb. who needs it

DOWN
1 to give sb. the idea to do sth.
2 the organ that covers the outside of your body
3 lesbian, gay, bisexual and transgendered
5 a group of people who share the same ideas or aims
6 to pull sth. into pieces

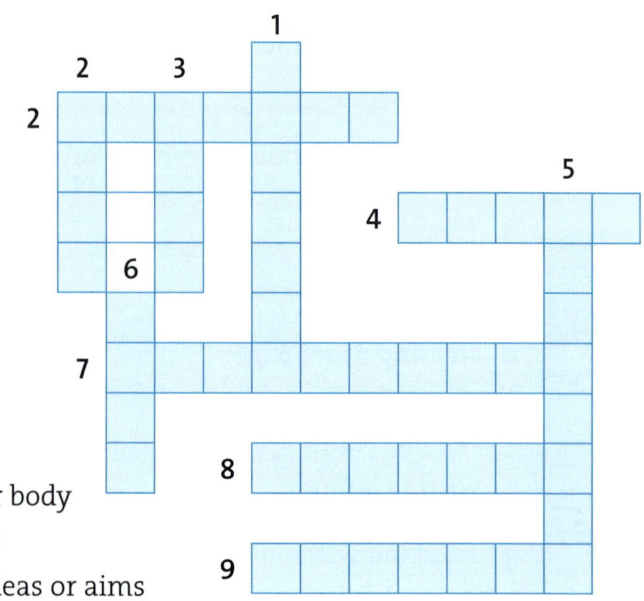

SB pp. 38-39

1 Check your vocabulary

a Complete this paragraph from a book about Native Americans.

Native Americans are the ______________ people of the United States. Many ______________ about Native Americans are not true. For example, only about a third live on ______________. Most Native Americans don't wear traditional dress every day, although many wear their hair in ______________. A headdress made of ______________ is a sacred thing worn by some tribes, especially by the tribal ______________. These are older tribe ______________ who know a lot about the traditions and culture of the tribe and give advice to others.

b Use one word from each box to make the caption for each picture.

driving • quotation • health • gun • break • drop out of	control • school • down • licence • care • marks

____

____

____

____

____

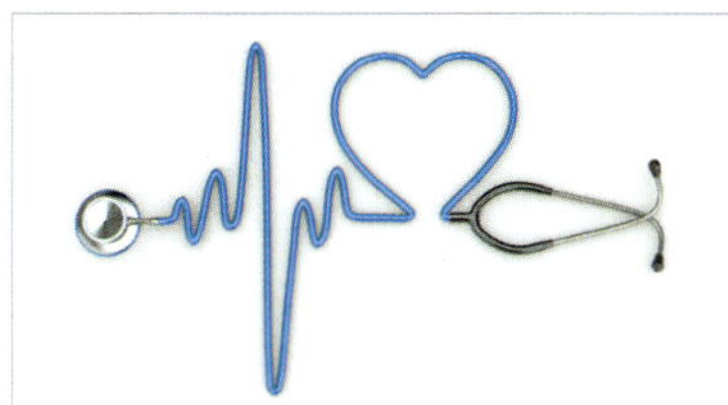
____

2 Check your language

a Complete the *if*-sentences with the right form of each verb.

1 Emma González *would like* (like) it if the United States ______________ (ban) guns.

2 It's hard to ______________ (do) online research if you ______________ (not have) a computer at home.

3 Grace ______________ (spread) more awareness, if she *gives* (give) more presentations about the Kewa pueblo across the country.

4 The Choctaw boy's mother thought that if the family ______________ (take) blankets from the soldiers, they ______________ (get) sick.

b Complete each sentence with *each other* or a reflexive pronoun.

1 She didn't prepare ________________ for this debate topic at all!
2 You need to listen to ________________ carefully during a debate.
3 I'm not very good at expressing ________________ when debating this topic.
4 The other team hurt ________________ in the debate with that silly argument.
5 I'd like you all to help ________________ prepare for the debate.

3 Check your mediation skills

You're discussing a film with your American friend. Give your opinion and ask questions in English.

1 Sag ihr, dass dir der Film sehr gut gefallen hat.
____.
2 Sag ihr, dass du die Kameraführung toll gefunden hast, besonders die Nahaufnahmen.
____.
3 Frag sie, wie sie die letzte Szene gefunden hat.
____?
4 Sag ihr, dass du anderer Meinung bist.
____.
5 Frag sie, warum sie den Film anderen empfehlen würde.
____?

4 Check your speaking

a Complete this presentation with suitable words and phrases.

Good ________________ everyone! Today I'm going to ____________ ____________ the film *Dances with Wolves*. ____________, I'm going to tell you about the plot. ____________, I'll ____________ if Native Americans are shown realistically in the film. ____________, I'll give my personal ____________ of the film.

In the film, which takes place during the Civil War[1] a soldier named John Dunbar hurts his leg very badly, so a doctor wants to cut it off. Here you ____________ a photo of Dunbar from the film. The soldier doesn't want to live with one leg and tries to commit ____________. He doesn't die and a better doctor saves his leg. Dunbar asks to go to the West, where he meets a ____________ of Lakota Native ____________. He decides to leave his old life to live with them. They give him the name Dances with Wolves. He falls in love with a white woman who also lives with the tribe. ...

b Practise giving the presentation.

[1] Civil War Bürgerkrieg

1 Describing people • Clothes • In a shop

Describe the picture in at least four sentences. Use the simple present to describe things, people and facts and the present progressive to describe what is happening and what the people are doing.

LF 1 → SB p. 136

Simple present	Present progressive
The store sells a lot of cool clothes.	*The woman at the counter is buying a blue jacket.*
______________________	______________________
______________________	______________________
______________________	______________________
______________________	______________________
______________________	______________________
______________________	______________________

2 Parts of the body • Health

Ed and Taylor are waiting at the school nurse's office. Complete their conversation. Use the present perfect or the present perfect progressive.

LF 3 → SB p. 139

Ed: Hi Taylor! **(1)** *Have you been waiting* (you; wait) here long?

Taylor: I **(2)** *'ve/have been* (be) here for about 20 minutes.

Ed: Aren't you feeling well?

Taylor: No, my stomach **(3)** ______________ (hurt) all day. What's wrong with you?

Ed: I **(4)** ______________ (have) a sore throat since yesterday. But it's worse now.

Taylor: **(5)** ______________ (you; drink) enough?

Ed: Yes ..., I **(6)** ______________ (fill) my bottle three times today.

Nurse: Taylor Davis, that's the second time I **(7)** ______________ (call) your name!

Taylor: Sorry! I **(8)** ______________ (talk) to Ed and I didn't hear you!

3 Places in the city • Asking for directions

a Put the words in the right order to ask questions.

1 tell / you / could / me / the way / to 5th Avenue / ?

____

2 route / take / should / we / which / to Queens / ?

____

3 to a Broadway show / you / have / ever / been / ?

____

4 do / we / get / how / to the museum / ?

____

5 blocks / how many / is / it / to the hotel / ?

____

6 Ellis Island / want / you / to go / do / to / ?

____

b What would you like to know about the NYC sight in the photo? Write two questions.

____

____

____

____

10 **c** Vincent is getting directions from his mobile phone in NYC. Find him on the map, listen and draw the route he takes. Where does he go?

____

d Ask your partner where she/he is on the map and where she/he wants to go. Give her/him directions. Take turns.

4 Booking a room

11 Alison wants to book a room for her holiday in NYC. Listen to her phone call. Are the sentences true or false? Tick (✔) the correct answers.

	true	false
1 Alison doesn't want to book online.	☐	☐
2 Alison wants to stay for five nights.	☐	☐
3 Only deluxe rooms are still free.	☐	☐
4 All the rooms have a bathtub.	☐	☐
5 The receptionist is friendly.	☐	☐
6 Alison books a standard room.	☐	☐

A changing world

Unit 3

Words and pictures

1 Detroit: Past and present

12 **a Complete the sentences using information from the interview with Mack.**

Detroit: past

1 Mack's great-grandfather worked on an ____________ line in one of the first car ____________.

3 There were once 50 ____________ on Isle Royale.

5 There were a lot of ____________ houses in the city.

7 ____________ music was created here in the 1980s.

Detroit: present

2 ____________ now do many jobs that people used to do.

4 The national park is bringing new ones here because there were ____________ ____________ moose[1].

6 Now ____________ are working to rebuild them for families who need homes.

8 There are fantastic DJs at the Movement electronic ____________ festival.

[1] moose Elch

b Match the two halves of the sentences to explain why things changed.

1 Workers in the car factories lost their jobs because ☐

2 Many workers then moved out of Detroit because ☐

3 The neighbourhoods became less safe because ☐

4 Isle Royale is bringing in new wolves because ☐

5 Teenagers started volunteering in the park because ☐

a gangs and drug addicts moved into the empty houses.

b they wanted to protect the environment.

c the park wants to control the number of moose.

d they wanted to live near the new factories.

e factories started using robots.

12 **c Listen to the podcast and check your answers to a and b.**

SB pp. 44–45

Smart technology

1 Tech talk

Use each word on the right to form a word from the same word family that fits in the space on the same line. You can find the words on SB pp. 46–47.

1 My smartphone is ______________ to my car.	CONNECTION
2 A drone ______________ goods in the air.	TRANSPORT
3 Codes ____________ other people from getting your data.	PREVENTION
4 New technology even makes car __________ more comfortable.	TO SIT
5 We couldn't __________ all of the problems.	SOLUTION
6 ____________ is very important to Mack when using smart technology.	PRIVATE
7 Many people worry about the ____________ of this app.	SECURE
8 These ____________ react to every little movement!	TO SENSE

SB pp. 46–47

2 What's the problem?

Circle the correct word in each phrase.

1 The *batterie* / *battery* / *batteries* has to be charged.

2 The *speaker* / *sneaker* / *speaking* is too loud.

3 There's no *spaces* / *space* / *place* on the floor.

4 I can't *onlock* / *unblock* / *unlock* the door.

5 The *windscreen* / *windstopper* / *windsheet* is broken.

6 There isn't a *roof* / *pillow* / *blanket* on the bed.

7 There's no lift for people with *unabilities* / *disablements* / *disabilities*.

SB pp. 46–47

3 Smart technology

a The letters in these verbs are mixed up. Write the correct words.

1 weak pu	__________	5 sprontart	__________
2 ropmarg	__________	6 clonuk	__________
3 cerude	__________	7 hersa	__________
4 crakt	__________	8 lovse	__________

b How can smart technology help us? Fill in the correct forms of the verbs from a.

1 Omar ______________ his fitness with a smartwatch.

2 Robots _____________ problems in the factory.

3 Katie's smart pillow ______________ her up every morning.

4 Self-driving trucks _________________ goods in Arizona.

5 I can ______________ my car with an app if I lose the key.

6 Alex worries that companies will _____________ his private information.

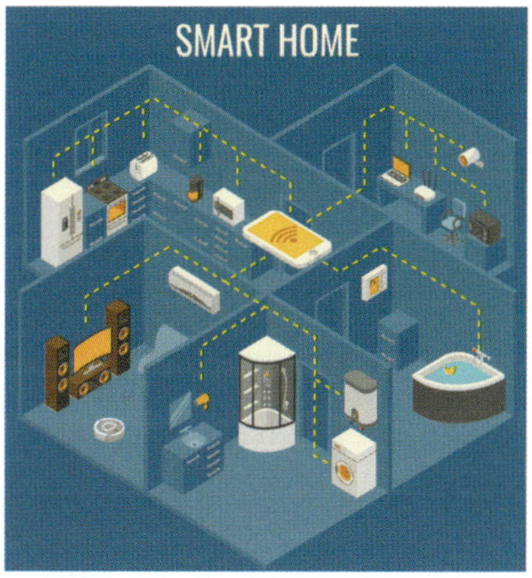

7 A smart fridge that helps you use all of your food can ______________ rubbish.

8 You can ________________ each machine differently with this app. SB pp. 46–47

13 **4 LISTENING The Smidge**

Listen to the ad and make notes to answer the questions. SB pp. 46–47

1 What kind of appliance is the ad for? ______________________________

2 What does the ad say that the Smidge will make easier (3 aspects)?

____

3 What can you check with the inside cameras (3 aspects)?

____

4 What can the Smidge track? ______________________________

5 What do you have to do before the Smidge can order food for you?

____

6 How can the Smidge help reduce your food rubbish?

____

7 How are your data and privacy protected? ______________________________

5 WRITING Silent conversation SB pp. 46–47

Write a sentence about a smart technology you use and swap papers. Your partner writes a question about the product and gives the paper back. Answer the question and swap papers again. Write three questions and answers. The phrases in the box can help you.

I use a ... • I use it to ... • It's useful because ... • One advantage / disadvantage is that ... • I wish ...

What do you use ... for? • Why do you like it? • What are its advantages? • How do you ... with it?

How things are made

1 Smart windscreens

Are the verbs in the active or passive form of the present tense? Tick (✓) A or P.

SB pp. 48-49

	A	P
1 Some new cars are built with smart windscreens.	☐	☐
2 These windscreens have functions to keep you safe.	☐	☐
3 They make a sound if you start to drive off the road.	☐	☐
4 Sensors are included in the windscreens.	☐	☐
5 They stop the car before you hit another car.	☐	☐
6 The windscreens are used for information services too.	☐	☐
7 They show you driving directions or petrol stations in the area.	☐	☐
8 If they are broken, smart windscreens have to be repaired by experts.	☐	☐

2 A short history of telephones

Write *was* or *were* to make verbs in the passive form of the simple past.

SB pp. 48-49

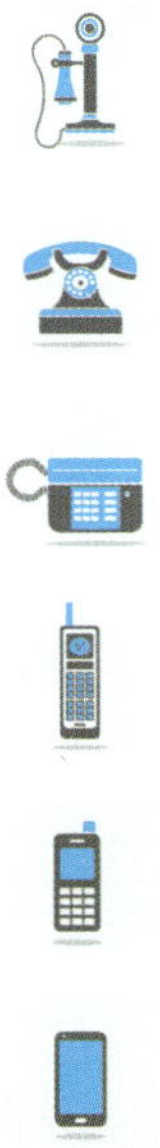

1876	1 The first telephone call ________ made by Alexander Graham Bell.
1877	2 The first telephone line ________ completed in Massachusetts.
1892	3 A telephone service ________ started between NY and Chicago.
Early 1900s	4 Pay phones ________ put in public places in the US.
1946	5 The first car phones ________ used.
1970s	6 The first wireless phones ________ sold.
1984	7 The first mobile phone ________ bought for $4000.
1994	8 Smartphones ________ invented.

3 Taking photos: then and now

Complete the sentences in the passive form of the simple present or simple past.

SB pp. 48-49

100 years ago	50 years ago	Today
Photos **(1)** ________ ________ (take) by a professional photographer. The person in the photo **(2)** ________ (tell) to stand still and smile.	Photos **(3)** ________ ________ (print) at a photo lab. That took a few days. If your photo didn't look good, it couldn't be improved.	Most photos **(4)** ________ (take) with digital cameras. Photos **(5)** ________ (share) in seconds with friends and family. Red eyes and other problems **(6)** ________ ________ (solve) quickly and easily.

Virtual reality

1 MEDIATION Virtual reality centre

Your mother's American friend is visiting you with her daughter Jordi. You want to take Jordi to a new virtual reality centre that has opened in your town. Look at the website together, tell her about the centre and answer her questions. SB p. 50

Virtual Reality in Bayern erleben

Willkommen in Bayerns größtem und modernstem VR-Zentrum. Hier kannst du virtuelle Realität auf zwanzig VR-Flächen in zehn Räumen erleben. Jeder Raum bietet Platz für bis zu fünf Spieler.

Für jeden die richtige Erfahrung: Egal was du für ein virtuelles Erlebnis suchst, wir haben das Richtige für dich. Kämpfe in einem intergalaktischen Krieg, gestalte dein Traumhaus, schwimm im tiefen Meer, besuche exotische Städte: Die Auswahl ist riesig. Und wer bei seinen Freunden nur zuschauen möchte, darf das natürlich auch, mit einem erfrischenden Getränk von unserer Bar.

Neueste Technik: Die tolle Grafik lässt das Erlebnis realistisch wirken. Ob Zuschauer oder Spieler, jeder in deiner Gruppe erhält einen kabellosen Kopfhörer und ein Mikrofon, damit ihr problemlos beim Spielen miteinander kommunizieren könnt. Spieler tragen natürlich ein VR-Headset.

Hygiene: Sauberkeit wird bei uns großgeschrieben! Die Geräte werden nach jeder Nutzung gründlich gereinigt.

Preise: Eine Stunde kostet 50 € für bis zu fünf Spieler/Gäste.

You: There's a new virtual reality centre in our town. Would you like to go?

Jordi: I'm not sure. What can you do there?

You: You put on a special headset and do different virtual activities. You can **(1)** ________ in an intergalactic war, ____________________ , ____________________ ____________ , or ________ exotic ________ .

Jordi: Do you play by yourself or with other people?

You: **(2)** ____ .

Jordi: That sounds like fun! What kind of equipment do you wear?

You: **(3)** ____ .

Jordi: What are the graphics like?

You: The website says **(4)** ____________________________________ .

Jordi: Do they clean their equipment? I don't want to get ill from putting something on my face that a lot of other people have used!

You: It says that they **(5)** ____________________________________ .

Jordi: Let's go! Oh, wait ... how much does it cost?

You: **(6)** ____ .

Jordi: Do you have any friends who could come with us?

Radio programmes

14 1 LISTENING Something for everyone

a Each member of Mack's family is listening to a different radio station in the morning. Listen and write down the correct letter next to each family member. Be careful: Use each letter only once.

A a weather report • B classical music • C techno music • D Detroit news • E a quiz show • F an interview • G a public service announcement • H celebrity news • I world news

1 Mack ____
2 Mack's mother ____
3 Mack's father ____
4 Mack's uncle ____
5 Mack's grandfather ____
6 Mack's grandmother ____

b What are the radio programmes about? Listen again and match the programmes with the topics. There are two topics you don't need.

1 Detroit news ☐
2 the quiz show ☐
3 the interview ☐
4 the public service announcement ☐

a The week's news
b This year's auto show
c Driving and texting
d New car technology
e What fun it is to text
f The cost of broken windscreens

SB p. 51

15 2 LISTENING Detroit today podcast

a Listen to the podcast. Are the statements true or false? Tick (✓) the correct boxes.

	true	false
1 Starting next year, the NAIAS will take place in the summer.	☐	☐
2 Until now, the show always took place at the beginning of the year.	☐	☐
3 The Detroit Auto Show is the most important auto show in the USA.	☐	☐
4 One reason for changing the date is the weather.	☐	☐
5 In the summer, customers have the chance to test the companies' cars.	☐	☐
6 Car companies saved money by taking part in a show in the winter.	☐	☐
7 Car companies aren't interested in organizing events to show their cars.	☐	☐
8 Organizers hope that more people and media will come to the summer show.	☐	☐
9 People are also more likely to do some sightseeing in Detroit in the summer.	☐	☐

b Correct the wrong sentences.

SB p. 51

____

____

____

____

Old and new

1 New treasures from old things

a These teens are reusing old things. Complete the sentences with the correct participles from the tables below.

1 While ____________ to school today, I discovered this bookcase next to a rubbish bin.

2 ____________ around with my cousin, I found some cool old clothes in our cellar.

3 ____________ one in a store, I decided to make my own bottle with lights in it.

4 ____________ to reuse my old jeans, I made this bag for my tablet.

5 ____________ with my sister, I made flowers from old news-papers.

6 ____________ old bottles, I make pencil holders for my desk.

7 ____________ a lot of old magazines, I cut them up to make birthday cards.

8 When ____________, I always save eggshells[1] to make tiny flower pots.

[1] **eggshell** Eierschale

1	a waking	b working	c walking
2	a Looking	b Liking	c Linking
3	a Saving	b Selling	c Seeing
4	a Wanting	b Wearing	c Hating

5	a Working	b Taking	c Fighting
6	a Reusing	b Drinking	c Needing
7	a Hating	b Holding	c Having
8	a eating	b cooking	c shopping

b Look at the sentences from a. Does each participle give extra information, a reason, or information about when the action happened? Tick (✓) the correct boxes.

SB pp. 52-53

	1	2	3	4	5	6	7	8
extra information								
reason								
information about the time								

The LOOK AT LANGUAGE box on SB p. 52 can help you with present participle constructions.

Writing a product review

1 WRITING New fitness tracker

a You ordered a new fitness tracker online. You've made some notes about the tracker. Before you write your review, decide if each point is positive or negative and put a tick (✓) in the correct box.

		Positive	Negative
1	*Comfortable to wear*	☐	☐
2	*Difficult to use*	☐	☐
3	*Doesn't seem to be a good quality product that will last for a long time*	☐	☐
4	*Looks cool*	☐	☐
5	*Doesn't have latest technology*	☐	☐
6	*Sleep tracker didn't work at all*	☐	☐
7	*Smells like chemicals*	☐	☐
8	*The tracker doesn't always connect to the app*	☐	☐
9	*Wasn't very expensive*	☐	☐

b How many stars would you give this product? Think about how many positive and negative points were in the list above. Colour in the number of stars. ☆ ☆ ☆ ☆ ☆

c Write your product review (100–120 words). Don't forget a heading. Include all of the points from a. Use adjectives and linking words.

Make your review more interesting with information like
- when and where you bought it
- what you use it for
- if it's better or worse than other fitness trackers you've tried

SB p. 54

Giving feedback on writing

1 SPEAKING AND WRITING A product review

a **Your friend Tenisha loves her new smart speaker. Read her review and give your feedback using the checklist below.**

The world's best smart speaker!

I realy love this speaker! I bought it in purpel and it looks grate. All of my frends think it's totally cool. The speeker works perfektly. The sound is amazing, even when I play my music LOUD, although the speaker is so small. Also, it always understands me when I talk to it.

I use the speaker for lots of things: it wakes me up in the morning with music and tells me what the wether is like. Sometimes I ask it to tell me jokes. My parents have a smart speeker in the kitchen and in their bedroom, so we use them to talk to each other from different rooms. That's grate because we don't have to shout anymore!

In addition, it was extremely eazy to connect to my phone: it only took about three minutes!

FEEDBACK CHECKLIST		
Content	**Yes/No**	**Comments**
Is the review easy to understand?	____	____________________
Is there enough information on the product?	____	____________________
Is the opinion of the writer clear?	____	____________________
Language	**Yes/No**	**Comments**
Does the writer use different adjectives?	____	____________________
Are the ideas joined with linking words?	____	____________________
Is the grammar correct?	____	____________________
Are spelling and punctuation correct?	____	____________________

b **Tenisha has also asked her friend Jo to give her feedback on her review. Unfortunately, Jo isn't very good at giving feedback. What could he say differently? Rewrite his feedback.** SB p. 55

> Your spelling is terrible! It makes the review hard to understand. And you need to give more information. The punctuation and grammar are OK, though.

Giving feedback
1. Say what was good.
2. Say what your partner can improve.
3. Give examples.

____

____

____

____

____

____

____

____

America's national parks

1 READING The changing face of national parks

a Using information from the article on SB pp. 56–57, write two ...

1 types of wildlife in America's national parks ____________ ____________
2 types of extreme weather in the US ____________ ____________
3 national parks ____________ ____________
4 extreme sports you can do in national parks ____________ ____________
5 types of bears in America's national parks ____________ ____________

b Tick (✓) the correct answers with information from the article.

1 Death Valley is dangerous because of ...	☐ its wildlife.	☐ its high temperatures.	☐ its natural disasters.
2 Climbers typically need ... to climb El Capitan.	☐ two hours	☐ two days	☐ four days
3 Extreme sports ...	☐ are bad for the environment.	☐ can cause accidents.	☐ are very safe.
4 Dylan McWilliams was attacked ...	☐ by a black bear.	☐ by a brown bear.	☐ in his tent.
5 Dylan ...	☐ played dead.	☐ fought back.	☐ caught the bear.
6 Rising air and water temperatures come from ...	☐ droughts.	☐ extreme weather.	☐ global warming.
7 The number of salmon has been reduced because of ...	☐ fishing.	☐ the diet of the Inuit.	☐ warmer water.

c Find and highlight words with these meanings in the puzzle. The words can go across (→), down (↓), or diagonally (↘). Don't highlight other words in the puzzle.

1 an animal that moves slowly and lives on land
2 the usual weather in a place
3 to be a danger to something
4 to become higher or larger
5 quiet and not violent
6 the way that somebody acts
7 a lot of water covering an area that is usually dry
8 a long time with little or no rain
9 a large water animal with front legs and a strong tail

X	Y	B	T	H	R	E	A	T	E	N	O	S	C
P	F	N	E	O	B	M	I	L	C	F	B	A	L
E	R	S	H	H	X	V	O	P	Q	L	O	I	I
A	T	M	A	N	A	T	E	E	Z	O	U	E	M
C	L	R	R	D	E	V	W	Q	B	O	A	R	A
E	K	J	I	C	N	H	I	G	D	D	S	U	T
F	A	L	S	I	H	D	R	O	U	G	H	T	E
U	Y	X	E	C	V	B	N	N	U	Q	W	A	R
L	D	T	O	R	T	O	I	S	E	R	F	N	T

d Write the word that goes with each definition.

SB pp. 56–57

1 Check your vocabulary

a Complete the sentences.

Radio DJs wear h________ on their ears and talk into a m________. Radio s________ don't just play music – they also report the news and play adverts and public service a________. The music on the radio is r________ in a studio.

b Write the missing words and definitions.

Word	Definition
1 to repair	________
2 ________	so important that you must do or have it
3 cotton	________
4 pocket	________
5 ________	a thing with teeth that you use to close bags
6 salmon	________

2 Check your language

a Rewrite the underlined parts of each sentence about recycling without the participle forms.

Example: Having many old objects, he decided to make art out of them. = Because he had many old objects, ...

1 After seeing a bookcase on the pavement, I called my friend and we carried it to my house. ________

2 Wanting to recycle a glass bottle, I put some pretty Christmas lights in it.

____

3 Taking a small stick, we put little pieces of old newspapers around it to make flowers.

____

4 Using a knife, I carefully cut around the plastic bottle. ________

b Complete the sentences with the passive form of the simple present or the simple past.

Before fridges **(1)** ________ (invent), iceboxes **(2)** ________ (use) to keep food cold. Ice **(3)** ________ (take) to people's houses by a horse and wagon. Iceboxes **(4)** ________ (make) of wood, with metal on the inside walls. Food **(5)** ________ (keep) cold inside by the ice.

Today, of course, our food **(6)** ________ (cool) by modern fridges that use electricity. Instead of ice, frozen food **(7)** ________ (transport) to many people's houses.

16

3 Check your listening

Listen and write down the missing words on the right.

1 Alaska is the ... state of the US. ______

2 Lake Clark is one of the ... national parks in the US. ______

3 The park protects landscapes, ... and people. ______

4 Lake Clark isn't ... by many natural disasters. ______

5 Lightning has caused ... in the park. ______

6 It is very ... to get to the park. ______

7 Brad and Cindy Levine like the park because it isn't very ... ______

8 They are most interested in seeing ... ______

9 There is a large population of red ... in the park. ______

4 Check your writing

Mack has written a review of a new video game. Circle the most suitable adjectives and linking words.

Big disapointment ★★★☆☆

I have to say that I'm really disappointed with the video game *Underground Life 6*. The only reason I'm giving it three stars is because the graphics are very **(1)** latest / realistic. The world is very **(2)** big / proper and a lot of fun to discover. **(3)** But / Therefore as **(4)** beautiful / virtual as it looks, there are a lot of problems with this game.

Firstly, this isn't like the other *Underground Life* games. The beginning of the game is **(5)** easy / hard to understand and leaves too much information out. You have to play a lot of short games that are all very **(6)** similar / organic to get to the next level. **(7)** In addition / Although, you really have to buy **(8)** extra / sustainable weapons. **(9)** And / So if you don't buy them, you're not **(10)** tall / strong enough to win fights.

Secondly, the game didn't always work with my system. A few times I had to start the game over. Sometimes **(11)** new / difficult characters suddenly appear and then quickly disappear. I hope they repair the problems soon!

Thirdly, **(12)** although / because the graphics are **(13)** great / colourful, the sound is **(14)** tasty / terrible! Without headphones, I couldn't understand what the characters were saying. And the background music is really **(15)** annoyed / annoying.

(16) Overall / However, I can't recommend this game. Try one of the other *Underground Life* games instead – they're a lot better!

Giving short talks

17

1 LISTENING An example of a short talk

You are going to give a short talk. Before you begin planning it, listen to Karla giving a short talk about something she is very interested in. Answer the following questions.

1 What is her talk about? ______________________

2 What phrase does Karla use to introduce her topic? ______________________

____

3 Which of these things does she mention? Tick (✔) the four correct boxes.

☐ blondies	☐ brownies	☐ pies	☐ bagels
☐ muffins	☐ scones	☐ cupcakes	☐ cookies

4 What is difficult about the following three things?

English recipes: ______________________

measuring things: ______________________

the ingredients[1]: ______________________

5 What phrase does Karla use to call attention to her photos? ______________________

6 In what order does Karla show these photos? Number the boxes.

☐ measuring cups

☐ brown sugar

☐ a recipe for cupcakes

☐ baked goods

7 How is her talk structured? What does she talk about …

at the beginning? ______________________

in the main part? ______________________

at the end (to sum up)? ______________________

2 Preparing your talk

You are also going to give a short (two-minute) talk about a topic you're interested in.

a **First choose a topic, for example a hobby, a pet, your family, your favourite band, etc.**

My topic: ______________________

[1] **ingredient** Zutat

b Make notes: what's important about this topic? You can use headings or make a mind map.

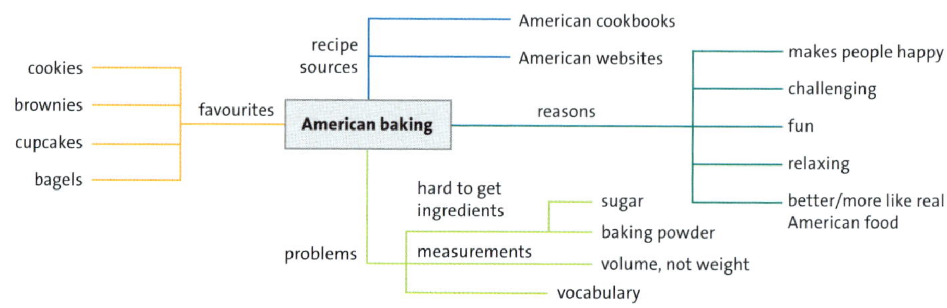

c Prepare notes for your talk.
- Structure your talk: beginning, main part and end.
- Find pictures and other media to help people understand your talk. Use either your own pictures or ones from Creative Commons and give the source.
- Write your notes neatly on a piece of paper or cards. Highlight the main points.

3 Practising and giving your talk

a Practise your talk with your notes from 2c in front of the mirror or film your talk. Then ask a friend or family member to watch you practise and fill in the feedback form.

Remember to ...	Remember not to ...
• Look at the class and smile • Speak clearly and confidently • Use your media to bring your talk to life	• Read from your notes: just look at the main points • Move around too much

You ...	Great!	Good	OK
presented the topic in a clear and interesting way.	☐	☐	☐
gave a good introduction and ending and presented information in a logical order.	☐	☐	☐
chose pictures/audio/objects well; they supported the talk.	☐	☐	☐
gave a good amount of information: not too much, not too little.	☐	☐	☐
spoke clearly and fluently.	☐	☐	☐
communicated thoughts and opinions clearly.	☐	☐	☐

b Use the feedback to practise your talk again.

c Give your talk to the class.

4 Talking about yourself

Imagine you are joining a group of volunteers for a community project of your choice.

a Prepare a one-minute talk about yourself, using the list of questions below. Make notes.

What's your name? • Do you have any pets? • How old are you? / When is your birthday? • What are your hobbies? • Where were you born? • Why do you want to volunteer? • Where do you live? / Who do you live with? • What are you good at?

b Give your talk to the class.

Black lives

Unit 4

Words and pictures

1 Famous couples

Match the women from Kelisha's scrapbook with their husbands.

1	Michelle Obama	☐ ☐	a	Shaun (Jay-Z)	d	44th President of the USA
2	Coretta Scott King	☐ ☐	b	Barack	e	musician and businessman
3	Beyoncé Knowles-Carter	☐ ☐	c	Martin Luther	f	civil rights leader

SB pp. 60–61

2 READING Short biographies

a Partner A: Read this short biography of Martin Luther King.
Partner B: Look at page 72.

Dr. Martin Luther King Jr. was born in Atlanta, Georgia in 1929. He fought for civil rights his whole life. He believed that the best way to change laws was by protesting without violence.
When King was a teenager in the American South, segregation was still the law there, also at the schools King went to. He finished high school at the age of 15 and went to a college for black students. He then studied to become a minister, which is the leader of a church. He married Coretta Scott in Boston; they had four children together.
King came back to the South to work in a church in Alabama. There he worked for civil rights, leading a protest against buses in Montgomery after Rosa Parks was arrested[1] in 1955 for not giving her seat to a white man. During the protest, King was arrested and his house was attacked. After 382 days, the highest court in the US decided that segregation on buses was against the law.
Between 1957 and 1968, King travelled over six million miles, giving speeches against discrimination. He also wrote five books. In 1963, he took part in the March on Washington, where he gave his famous "I Have a Dream" speech. King won the Nobel Peace Prize in 1964 for his work for the civil rights movement. At the time, he was the youngest person who had ever won this award.
On April 4, 1968, King was standing on the balcony of his hotel room in Tennessee when he was shot and killed by a white man. To remember his life and work, Martin Luther King Jr. Day has been made a national holiday and is celebrated on the third Monday of January every year.

b Circle the correct word or phrase to complete each sentence about Martin Luther King.

1 King tried to change laws through *violent / peaceful / quiet* protest.
2 King attended a *segregated / northern / white* college.
3 After university, he worked at a church in *Boston. / Atlanta. / Alabama.*
4 In 1964, King became the *youngest / first black / only* person to ever win the Nobel Peace Prize.
5 King's life and work is celebrated *as a national holiday. / only in Tennessee. / mostly by African Americans.*

c Make notes on Martin Luther King. Then give a one-minute talk about him to your partner.

SB pp. 60–61

[1] **to be arrested** verhaftet werden

Black lives matter

1 READING Black lives matter

a Read the article about the shooting deaths of unarmed black men on SB pp. 62–63 again. What is true, false or not in the text? Tick (✓) the correct boxes.

	true	false	not in the text
1 A police officer named George Zimmerman shot Trayvon Martin.	☐	☐	☐
2 George Zimmerman said sorry to Trayvon's family.	☐	☐	☐
3 Tamir Rice's gun was just a toy.	☐	☐	☐
4 The police officer who shot Tamir knew that the gun was probably fake.	☐	☐	☐
5 The *Black Lives Matter* movement protests against racial profiling.	☐	☐	☐
6 Barack Obama says that he has also been the victim of racial profiling.	☐	☐	☐
7 The *Black Lives Matter* movement hasn't changed anything.	☐	☐	☐

b • Correct the wrong sentences.

____

____

____

c Answer the questions about the text.

1 Who started the *Black Lives Matter* movement and when?

____

2 What types of laws have been passed since 2015?

____

SB pp. 62–63

2 Protest slogans

Think of some slogans for the *Black Lives Matter* movement. Pick the best one and write it on the sign below. You can decorate it to make people notice it.

SB pp. 62–63

3 WORDS Crime and justice

Find a word or phrase in the text on SB pp. 62–63 with the same or similar meaning as each of the words below.

SB pp. 62-63

1 aim at sb.	______	5 not real	______
2 murdered	______	6 unprotected	______
3 emergency number	______	7 demonstration	______
4 weapon	______	8 rule	______

4 More victims

18

a LISTENING Listen to the news story about another man who was killed by the police in the US. Fill in the information below. You do not have to write complete sentences.

1 First name: ______

2 Last name: ______

3 Lived in (city): ______

4 What the situation was: ______

______

______

Mural of Freddie Gray by street art artist Nether and Brandon Ross, Baltimore 2015

5 What happened to him: ______

______

6 Who was responsible: ______

b Pick one of the tasks below.

1 Look at the list of unarmed black men killed by the police at the top of the article on SB p. 62. Use the internet to find out more about one of them and what happened to him. Write a short profile, including the following information:
- What was his name?
- Where did he live (city)?
- What was the situation?
- What happened to him?
- Who was responsible?
- What happened afterwards?
- Your opinion: Did the police officers make a mistake? Why or why not?

2 Use the internet to find out more about an organization that is working to fight racial injustice, for example *Black Lives Matter*, *Million Hoodies*, the *American Civil Liberties Union (ACLU)* or the *National Association for the Advancement of Colored People (NAACP)*. Write a short description of the organization, including the following information:
- When was the organization started?
- What are the goals of the organization?
- What does it do?
- How can people get involved?
- Your opinion: Is this organization helping? What else could be done?

SB pp. 62-63

Great achievements

1 Colin Kaepernick

Read the text. Then circle a verb with two objects in each highlighted part. Underline the two objects.

SB pp. 64-65

Before American sports events, everybody stands up for the national anthem[1]. If anybody sits, it's disrespectful. But in August 2016, football player Colin Kaepernick didn't stand up. He explained the reason to reporters. It was because black people were being racially profiled, hurt and killed by the police.

Kaepernick was born to a white mother and an African American father. His mother, who was only 19 when Colin was born, couldn't keep him. A white couple gave him a home.

After Kaepernick sat during several anthems, player Nate Boyer suggested a different solution to him. He recommended kneeling during the song. Kneeling showed respect but was still a sign of protest.

During the 2016–17 football season, many players from the 49ers and other teams also sat or knelt during the song. Athletes from other sports also showed Kaepernick support.

October 23, 2016 – Florida, US

With the beginning of the new football season in 2017, President Donald Trump brought the topic to the front pages again. Trump said that team owners should fire players who didn't stand for the national anthem, and that fans should walk out of stadiums in protest.

The reaction from football players came quickly. On the weekend after Trump's speech, over 200 players sat, knelt, or linked arms during the song. Some teams stayed off the field during the song. Many who sat or knelt were protesting Trump, rather than racism.

Colin Kaepernick left his team in March 2017. He was not taken by another team, although he is a very good player. But a company that sells popular sports clothes gave him a job advertising their products.

[1] **national anthem** Nationalhymne

2 What happened because of Colin Kaepernick's protest?

a Tick (✓) the the sentences with the correct position of objects. Both sentences may be correct.

1	☐ He sent Americans a message about racial profiling.	☐	He sent a message about racial profiling to Americans.
2	☐ His protests got him a lot of attention.	☐	His protests got a lot of attention to him.
3	☐ Many people wrote letters him.	☐	Many people wrote him letters.
4	☐ No other teams offered him a job.	☐	No other teams offered a job to him.
5	☐ Media reported Trump's ideas to their readers.	☐	Media reported their readers Trump's ideas.

b Circle the 'person object' in each sentence. Then rewrite the sentences in the simple past passive. Use the 'person object' as the subject of the new sentence.

SB pp. 64-65

1 A white couple gave Colin a home. ______

2 Other players showed Kaepernick support. ______

3 The company paid him a lot of money to be in adverts for sports clothes. ______

______

In New Orleans

19

1 LISTENING New Orleans culture

a Listen to the dialogues and match their number (1–6) with the correct picture (a–f).

a

b

c

d

e

f

b Listen again and make notes to answer the questions. SB p. 66

1 What food goes well with this dish? __________

2 Why is the girl happy to share? __________

3 What do you get if you order yours "dressed"? __________

4 Why didn't the woman make it herself? __________

5 What does the father like about this one? __________

6 Why doesn't the father want a big piece? __________

2 What's important to me?

a Write down three things, people or values that are important to you. How do you show their importance to you in everyday life?

Use the simple present to talk about things that are always true (like a value) or things that regularly happen.

1 __________ is/are important to me, so I __________

2 __________

____

3 __________

____

b SPEAKING Share something from 2a with a partner. Find more ideas for showing what's important to you in your life. SB p. 66

After Katrina

Actor Brad Pitt in New Orleans

1 READING Hurricane Katrina

a Here are four texts about Hurricane Katrina. Read them and match them with the statements 1–6 below. Choose the correct text (A–D) and write the letter on the line. The texts may be chosen more than once.

A When Hurricane Katrina hit New Orleans, thousands of people who hadn't left the city went to the Superdome sports stadium. The stadium had been used for shelter in other storms. After Katrina, the conditions got worse and worse. The wind blew two holes in the roof, so rain came in and the stadium field flooded. The toilets broke and the stadium smelled very bad because there was no water in the ladies' and men's rooms. There were no beds and nowhere for sick people to go ... and no doctors. Three people died. Many people reported crimes. Most people did not leave the stadium until 1st September, a week after the hurricane. Some people couldn't leave until 4th September.

B Thousands of people didn't leave their houses. Some were too old or sick, some didn't have transport, and some didn't believe that the hurricane would be so dangerous. After the flood walls broke, much of the city was under water. Many people couldn't get out of their houses. Some people went onto their roofs. Police officers, the army and volunteers went out in boats to find people and take them to safe places. Other people were saved by helicopter. Organizations like the Red Cross came to New Orleans and gave people food and health care. Thousands of people were taken to other towns and states.

C Many stars helped after the hurricane. Actor Sean Penn saved people in a boat, while Julia Roberts and John Travolta brought medicine with an organization run by talk show host Oprah Winfrey. Another talk show host, Ellen DeGeneres, who is from New Orleans, gave a new shop to a woman who had lost her business in the storm. Stars like George Clooney and Jay-Z gave money to help victims. Brad Pitt started an organization to build new houses for people whose homes were destroyed by Katrina and gave millions of dollars to the project.

D Since 2005, over 300 miles of new flood walls have been built. Old homes have been repaired and new homes finished. There are new schools and a new hospital. Even the Superdome was rebuilt ... and the city's football team won the Super Bowl in 2010. Thousands of people have moved back to the city. However, thousands of people have not. Some people were scared to go back, others didn't have enough money, a job or a place to live. The culture of New Orleans is still alive and well, including Mardi Gras, music and food.

1 Help in the form of action and money came from many famous people. ____

2 Thousands of people took shelter in this building, but the situation was terrible there. ____

3 Some people never went home again. ____

4 New structures and buildings have made New Orleans a better place to live. ____

5 People were saved by air and by water. ____

6 Some people didn't leave because they thought they would be safe at home. ____

b Read the *if*-sentences and tick (✔) yes or no to answer the questions.

1 If we had left the city before the hurricane, we wouldn't have had to go to the Superdome.
Did they leave the city before the hurricane? ☐ yes ☐ no
Did they have to go to the Superdome? ☐ yes ☐ no

2 If the toilets hadn't broken, the stadium wouldn't have smelled so bad.
Did the toilets break? ☐ yes ☐ no
Did the stadium smell bad? ☐ yes ☐ no

3 If she hadn't been so sick, she would have left her house.
Was she sick? ☐ yes ☐ no
Did she leave her house? ☐ yes ☐ no

c Use information from the texts on page 50 to complete the sentences.

Remember:
if-clause = past perfect • main clause = would/could/might (not) have + the past participle
If she had helped, we might have finished the job. • *I would have come if you had invited me.*

1 If people hadn't gone to the Superdome, *they might have* __________.
2 Rain wouldn't have come in the Superdome __________.
3 If the flood walls hadn't broken, __________.
4 If volunteers hadn't helped, __________.
5 More people would have gone back to the city __________.

d Write an *if*-sentence type 3 for each of the following situations.

1 I moved to Texas because my aunt offered to let me live with her.
I wouldn't have moved to Texas if my aunt hadn't offered to let me live with her.

2 The field flooded because it rained through the roof.
__________.

3 Thousands of people got food because the Red Cross came.
__________.

SB pp. 68–69

2 WORD FAMILIES Adjectives with *-ed* and *-ing*

Read each sentence and circle the correct word.

1 Sitting in the Superdome for days was very *depressed / depressing*.
2 My little brother was *bored / boring* because we didn't have any toys with us.
3 We were really *annoyed / annoying* because the family near us was so loud.
4 I was very *interesting / interested* in the plans for the new houses.

SB p. 69

Extreme storms

1 READING AND WORDS Staying safe in a tornado

a Read the poster. Highlight all words you don't know.

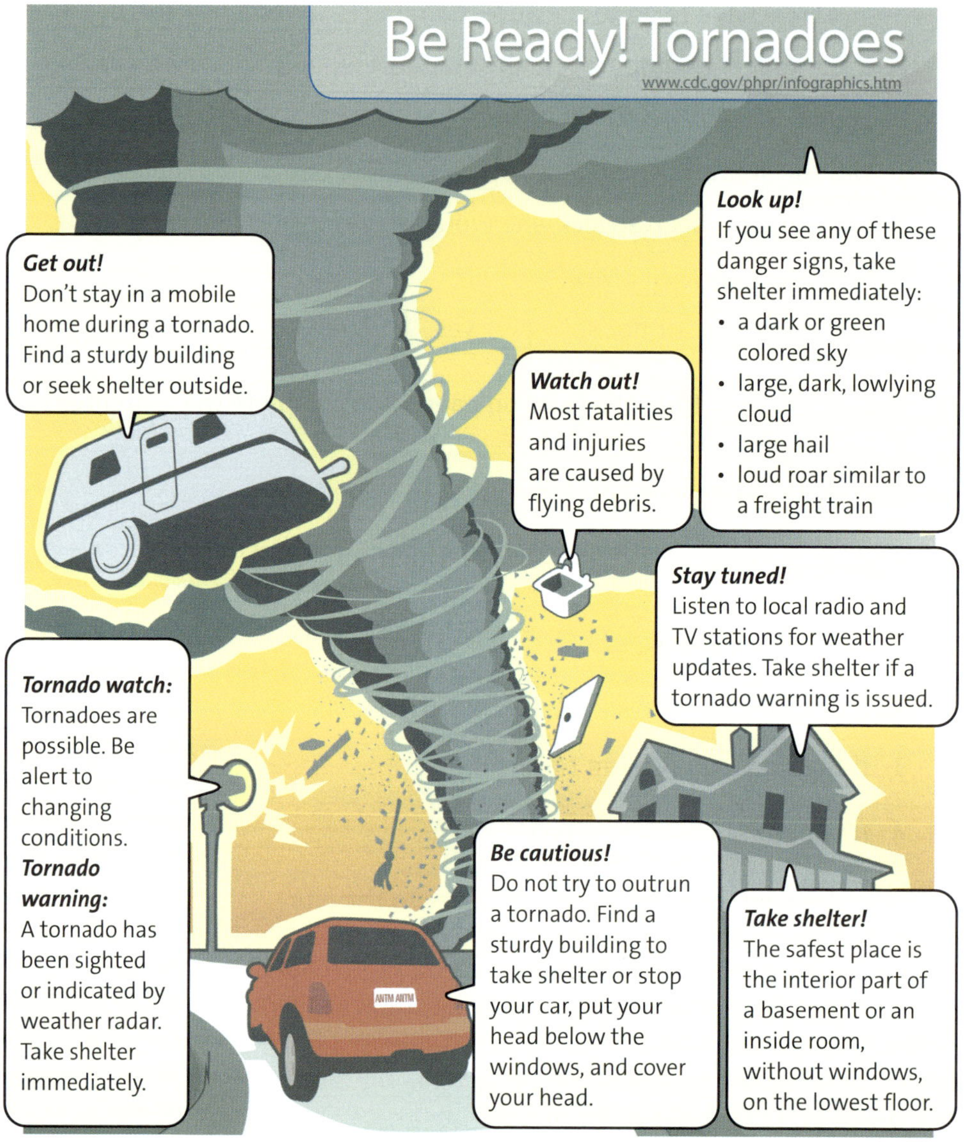

Source: Centers for Disease Control and Prevention

b Write the words you don't know in the table below. Tick (✔) any strategies that help you figure out the meaning. Write down what you think the meaning is. Then check in a dictionary and write down the meaning. Use another piece of paper if you need more space.

Word	Strategy					Meaning	
	picture/ heading	the situation	similar word	word family	compound word	possible meaning	dictionary meaning
sturdy	✔	✔					

c Use the prefixes in the box to make the opposites of words from the poster. Use a dictionary if you need one.

ex- • im- • out- • un-

SB p. 70

1 possible ◄► ____________
2 interior ◄► ____________
3 cover ◄► ____________
4 inside ◄► ____________
5 mobile ◄► ____________
6 safest ◄► ____________

An appointment at the doctor's

1 MEDIATION AND LISTENING Calling for an appointment

20

a You are calling the doctor's to make an appointment. Listen to the recording and answer the questions in German.

1 Was tut man in einem Notfall? ______

2 Was passiert, wenn man bei der ersten Ebene die zwei wählt? ______

______

3 Wofür wählt man die vier? ______

4 Welche Ziffer wählst du, wenn du ein Rezept brauchst? ______

5 Wie kann man eine Kopie von einem Dokument bekommen? ______

6 Wie kannst du die Optionen erneut anhören? ______

7 Welche Ziffernfolge muss man wählen, um auf Englisch einen Termin zu vereinbaren? ______

b Continue the conversation.

Receptionist: Hello, this is Elaine. Would you like to make or change an appointment?

You: Sage ihr, du würdest gerne einen neuen Termin vereinbaren. ______

______

Receptionist: What can the doctor do for you?

You: Sage, du hast Ohrenschmerzen. ______

Receptionist: I can offer you an appointment for today at three-thirty.

You: Sage zu und bedanke dich. ______

Receptionist: Can I have your name and date of birth, please?

You: Nenne deinen Namen und dein Geburtsdatum. ______

______

Receptionist: We'll see you this afternoon. Please bring your insurance documents. Goodbye.

You: Bestätige das und verabschiede dich. ______

2 SPEAKING At the doctor's

Partner A: Look at page 71. Partner B: Look at page 73.

SB p. 71

The Hate U Give

Angie Thomas

1 WORDS Words from the story

Match each word/phrase from the story on SB pp. 72–73 with its meaning.

1	Carnation (l. 15)	☐	a	that's private
2	One-fifteen (l. 37)	☐	b	the police officer's badge number
3	nunya (l. 39)	☐	c	aren't
4	gon' (l. 42)	☐	d	dead
5	ain't (l. 57)	☐	e	going to
6	gone (l. 91)	☐	f	the name of a street

SB pp. 72-73

2 What would you have done?

Say what you would or wouldn't have done. Use *if*-sentences type 3.

1 The police officer stopped Khalil's car.

If I had been the police officer, I wouldn't have stopped Khalil's car.

2 Khalil didn't give the police officer his documents quickly.

____

3 Khalil went back to the door of the car.

____

4 The police officer shot Khalil when he opened the door of the car.

____

5 Starr jumped out of the car to help Khalil.

____

SB pp. 72-73

3 Voices and silence

Voices and silence play important roles in this story. Look at the lines in the story given below. Which characters use their voice or are silent in that line? Why?

SB pp. 72-73

	Voice	Silence
Line numbers: 4–5 Character(s): ______	☐	☐
Why? ______		
Line number: 50 Character(s): ______	☐	☐
Why? ______		
Line number: 90 Character(s): ______	☐	☐
Why? ______		

1 Check your vocabulary

a Give an example from the unit of each of the following words.

1 segregation ______
2 civil war ______
3 victim ______
4 trial ______
5 scrapbook ______
6 sportsperson ______
7 seafood ______
8 vehicle ______

b Complete the sentences with words from *The Hate U Give*.

1 When he's talking to Starr, Khalil calls the police officer a f______.
2 The police officer points his f______ at Khalil to see his face.
3 He asks for p______ of Khalil's insurance.
4 Khalil gets the documents out of his w______.
5 Starr remembers the police officer's b______ number.
6 The police officer wears his hair in a b______ cut.
7 One-Fifteen has a s______ over his l______.
8 The police officer wants Starr to put her hands on the d______.
9 Khalil g______ after he's shot the second time.

2 Check your language

a Rewrite the sentences with *to*.

1 She threw me the beads. ______.
2 He gave her a costume. ______.

b Rewrite the sentences without to.

1 I brought a po' boy to her. ______.
2 We sent a king cake to them. ______.

c **Finish the *if*-sentences type 3 with your own ideas.**

1 If I hadn't eaten the seafood, ______________________.

2 She wouldn't have won a gold medal ______________________.

3 The law would never have been changed ______________________.

3 Check your mediation skills

What do you say in these situations in English?

1 Am Telefon fragst du, ob der Arzt morgen noch einen freien Termin hat.

____

2 Du sagst, dass du gegen Hunde allergisch bist.

____

3 Du fragst den Arzt, ob du Antibiotika brauchst.

____

4 Check your writing

Underline the thirteen mistakes in this scrapbook entry. Write the correct words on the right.

Serena Williams

In addition to being won of the greatest tennisplayers ever, Serena Williams is a big supporter of the Black Lives Matter moment. She was one of the first famous sportsperson to speak out about the killing of teenager Michael Brown. He has told other aktivists not to give up. Williams has also speaked about being worried that boys in her family could be victims from police shootings. She's not afraid to say what she thought!

Williams has winned more Grand Slam competitions then any other woman or man! Her sister Venus is also a grate player and they've won lots of game together.

1 Chores

Describe what happened while the kids in the Gomez family were doing their chores last week. Use the simple past or the past progressive of the verbs in the box. There are four verbs you don't need.

Look at LF 2 SB p. 137 for help on the use of simple past and past progressive.

break • burn • do • find • have • lock • look • ~~meet~~ • mow • set • start • take out • turn • vacuum • ~~walk~~ • write

1 Sergio and Sara *were walking* the dog when they *met* Emily.

2 Sara ____________ the floor when she ____________ a pound coin.

3 Sergio ____________ the dishes when he ____________ a glass.

4 Sofia ____________ herself out of the house while she ____________ the trash.

5 While Símon ____________ the table, his father ____________ the dinner.

6 It ____________ to rain while Sofia ____________ the grass.

2 Holidays

a Circle the correct words to complete Rana's email to her friend Neve.

Hi Neve!

I'm having the *great / greatest* holiday! Today we went to the *most cool / coolest* water park I've ever seen. The slides were even *longer / longest* than the ones at AquaFunLand … but also a little *more dangerous / dangerouser*. The water wasn't *as / so* warm as in AquaFunLand, but it was definitely *cleaner / more clean*. They had four diving boards: the *most low / lowest* one was just a one-metre board, but they had a high one that was three metres and a *higher / more high* one that was five metres. The *most high / highest* one was ten metres!

Tomorrow we're going to a museum. I think it will be a little less exciting *as / than* the water park.

See you soon!

Rana

b **Neve thinks that the water park sounds such fun that she has asked her father to take her family there too. Complete the *if*-sentences from Neve's answer to Rana's email.** LF 6 → SB pp. 142–143
LF 12 → SB pp. 150–151

1 If we ______________ (know) you were going there, we could have gone together!

2 If you ______________ (have) some photos of the park, please send them to me!

3 We ______________ (book) a room if the hotel isn't full.

4 We would stay in the hotel's best room if we ______________ (have) enough money.

5 The website says that the park ______________ (be) cheaper if you go in the winter.

6 If my mother's boss let her take a holiday, she ______________ (come) too.

7 My sister gets an ear infection if she ______________ (stay) in the water too long.

8 I ______________ (write) to you yesterday if I hadn't been so tired.

c **In her email to Neve, Rana said that her family was going to a museum the next day. Write an email from Rana to Neve describing her day at the museum. Be sure to write what kind of museum it was (art, history, science), how she liked it and why, what she saw and what she did there. Write about 130 words.**

3 A crazy weekend

a **Partner B: Look at page 75. Partner A: Ask your partner to give you words to fill each gap to make a silly story.**

That was ______________ (a/an + adjective) weekend! On Saturday, I woke up at ______________ (number between 1 and 12) o'clock. I ate some ______________ (a food) for breakfast with my ______________ (word for a family member). Then I fed my pet ______________ (type of animal). I had to do some ______________ (school subject) homework: it was really ______________ (adjective). I had plans to ______________ (infinitive verb) with my friend ______________ (name of a friend). I took the ______________ (type of vehicle) there. We had ______________ (a/an + adjective) day! The best part was when I ______________ (simple past verb) while we were ______________ (*ing*-form of a verb). The worst part was when we hurt our ______________ (body part, plural) while we were ______________ (*ing*-form of a verb).

b **Read the text to the class.**

In Canada

Unit 5

Words and pictures

1 Symbols of Canada

Search the internet for information about these symbols of Canada. Write a caption (1–2 sentences) for each one for Olivier's blog. The words and phrases in the box may help you.

to be called • bird • coin • to find • French • holiday • horse • lakes • national • nickname • police officer • to ride • song

1

moose

1 ______________________________

2

loon

Loonies

2 ______________________________

3

Canada Day

3 ______________________________

4
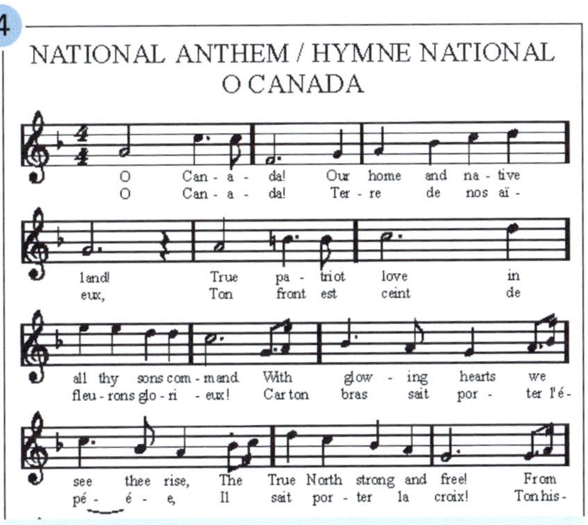

O Canada

5

mountie

5 ______________________________

4 ______________________________

SB pp. 78-79

21

2 LISTENING AND SPEAKING Canada quiz

Partner A: Look at page 73.

Partner B: Look at page 74.

SB pp. 78-79

The polar bear capital of the world

1 WORDS Wrong words

Underline the wrong word or phrase in each sentence.
Write the correct words from the text on SB pp. 80–81 on the right.

SB pp. 80-81

1 Churchill has a special bear alarm team. (paragraph A) ____________

2 Many ice bears walk through Churchill every year. (para. D) ____________

3 A man drove his car at the bear while blinking his lights. (para. A/F) ____________

4 Using your car hoop also helps frighten bears. (para. A) ____________

5 The bears are caught in a fall and then taken to prison. (para. C) ____________

6 Bears hunt for sea dogs on the Hudson Bay. (para. D) ____________

7 The ice melts earlier every year because of earth warming. (para. D) ____________

8 The bear packed Erin's head! (para. F) ____________

9 It tore off part of her head skin. (para. F) ____________

10 Bill and Erin lived over the attack. (para. F) ____________

2 WORDS An email about the attack

Erin is writing about the attack to her cousin in California. Use the right words from the box to complete the sentences. There are three words you don't need.

alert • attitude • autumn • bay • fear • frighten • immigration • kilos • local • migration • shovel • terrifying

Hi Rose,

I'm sure you've heard the news of my polar bear attack by now! It was the most ____________ thing that has ever happened to me. I was walking home from a party with my friends when a huge bear came running towards us and grabbed me! It must have weighed about 500 ____________ . I started screaming (of course!) and a ____________ man came out of his house and started hitting the bear with a ____________ . Other neighbours tried to ____________ it away with cars and gun shots, but then the police came and killed it. Usually you don't have to worry about polar bears too much, but it's November and the ____________ is their ____________ season. I'm not exactly living in ____________ now, and my ____________ towards polar bears hasn't changed, but maybe I'll come visit you in California until the season is over!

Love, Erin

SB pp. 80-81

3 READING AND LISTENING Numbers

a Find the numbers in the text on SB pp. 80–81.

1 The year in which Erin Greene was attacked ______
2 Bill Ayote's age at the time of the attack ______
3 The number of friends with Erin when she was attacked ______
4 The length of male polar bears ______
5 How heavy male polar bears are ______
6 The number of polar bears around Churchill ______
7 There are about this many more polar bears than people around Churchill ______
8 The distance between Churchill and the next town ______
9 The number of days polar bears stay in "prison" ______

22

b Listen to the podcast about polar bears and complete the text with the correct numbers.

There have been polar bears for ______ years. Today, there are ______ polar bears and as many as ______ live in Canada. Bears usually live to be about ______ years old. They can swim for at least ______ kilometres without stopping. They can smell animals that are ______ kilometres away. But, by the year 2050, their population could be reduced by ______.

SB pp. 80–81

4 READING Polar bears in town

Which heading goes best with which paragraph in the text on SB pp. 80–81? Match the headings (1–9) with the letters (A–F). There are three headings you don't need.

1 Favourite food ☐
2 Migration every year ☐
3 Flashing lights ☐
4 Daily danger ☐
5 Back to the wilderness ☐
6 Polar bear attack! ☐
7 Bears in the air ☐
8 Facts about polar bears ☐
9 Bear watching ☐

SB pp. 80–81

At adventure camp

1 Camping activities

a Circle the right verbs to form negative questions.

1 *Weren't / Aren't / Isn't* it beautiful here?

2 *Won't / Haven't / Hasn't* they help wash up?

3 *Don't / Won't / Can't* you want to go swimming?

4 *Isn't / Weren't / Wasn't* there some marshmallows in this bag?

5 *Haven't / Shouldn't / Hasn't* we hang our food in a tree?

6 *Wasn't / Isn't / Aren't* you going to put out the campfire?

7 *Didn't / Doesn't / Can't* you want to listen to the ghost stories?

23 b Listen and check your answers.

c Use negative questions to say it another way. SB pp. 82–83

1 I can't believe you have never been fishing! (ever) Haven't you ever been fishing?

2 I think they could carry that. (couldn't) ____________________

3 It's time for us to go home now. (shouldn't) ____________________

4 She said she would bring the hot dogs. ____________________

5 I thought they were going to come with us. ____________________

2 Confirming information about someone

Write down three more negative questions to ask a partner about herself/himself using different verbs and tenses. Then ask the questions.

1 Didn't you go to Canada last year?

2 ____________________

3 ____________________

4 ____________________

Some ideas for your questions:
- Don't you play …?
- Aren't you interested in …?
- Doesn't your family live in …?
- Haven't you seen/read/…?

SB pp. 82–83

3 Making lists

a Complete Olivier's list for preparing for his next camping trip with *make* or *do*.

b Make your own list, for example for your afternoon / the weekend / a party / a school project …

To (1) ________

- *(2) ________ research on camping sites*
- *(3) ________ a reservation*
- *(4) ________ sure the tent doesn't have any holes*
- *ask what kinds of sport we can (5) ________ there*
- *(6) ________ extra chores to pay for the trip!*

SB pp. 82–83

Asking follow-up questions

1 How was the camping trip?

a Madison, a girl from Olivier's class, is telling her mother about the camping trip. Put the dialogue in the right order (1–10).

☐	**Madison**	It was sunny almost every day. One day it rained, but that was actually good!
☐	**Mom**	I'm glad you had a good time. What did you do there?
☐	**Mom**	You mentioned cooking fish. Will you cook some for us soon?
☐	**Madison**	We went canoeing and fishing. I learned how to put up a tent and cook fish.
☐	**Mom**	That sounds exciting! How was the weather?
1	**Mom**	How was your camping trip?
☐	**Mom**	What exactly do you mean by that?
☐	**Madison**	We slept late and it was really nice to sit in the warm tent, chat and relax.
☐	**Madison**	Yes, sure I can do that. But you need to help, mom!
☐	**Madison**	It was great! We had a lot of fun.

24 b Now listen and check your answers.

c Practise the dialogue with a partner. SB p. 84

2 Favourite foods

Luka wants to know about Ji-min's favourite foods. Complete the dialogue with follow-up questions.

Ji-min: I enjoy eating more than cooking!

Luka: ____________________

Ji-min: Well, I really love Mexican food!

Luka: I don't know much about Mexican food. ____________________

Ji-min: A lot of it is spicy! They use tortillas a lot: they're thin pancakes made from corn flour.

Luka: ____________________

Ji-min: You eat them with meat, beans or vegetables.

Luka: Sounds good. ____________________

Ji-min: My favourite Canadian food is butter tarts. Yum!

SB p. 84

3 Butter tarts

Olivier joins Luka and Ji-min's conversation. Match the phrases in blue with their functions (A–C). More than one phrase can be used for a function.

1 **Olivier:** *You mentioned butter tarts, right?* ☐
2 **Ji-min:** Yes, I love them!
3 **Olivier:** *That's cool.* ☐ I know how to make them.
4 **Luka:** *What did you say?* ☐
5 **Olivier:** I know how to make them.
6 **Luka:** *Awesome!* ☐ Can you show me?

A	Show interest
B	Go back to a topic
C	Check understanding

Rodeo and relay

1 READING Rodeo fans

a Read the comic. Then underline the emphatic pronouns and circle the reflexive pronouns.

Emphatic pronouns emphasize a person or thing: *I don't eat meat* ***myself***. If you leave them out, the sentence still makes sense: *I don't eat meat*.

7

8

b Complete the sentences with the correct emphatic pronouns.

1 If the parents don't want to leave the rodeo, the kids can take the bus home ____________.

2 "I wasn't so interested in coming to the rodeo ____________."

3 Alyssa had saved the money to buy the ticket ____________.

4 The parents ____________ had never been to a rodeo.

5 "You chose these seats ____________!"

c Circle the right form of *be able to, be allowed to* or *have to* in each sentence.

1 The kids *were allowed to / were able to / had to* go to the rodeo.

2 At the rodeo, the family *was able to / was allowed to / had to* sit in the hot sun.

3 The kids *weren't allowed to / didn't have to / weren't able to* take the bus.

4 The family *wasn't allowed to / didn't have to / wasn't able to* go into the stadium early.

5 Alyssa *didn't have to / wasn't allowed to / wasn't able to* tell her family the real start time.

d Use one chunk from each box to make true sentences.

Babies • Gay people • I • People • We

weren't able to • weren't allowed to • will be able to • will be allowed to • will have to

drive alone when I'm 18. • fly to the moon until 1969. • go back to school after the summer holidays. • marry in most countries until recently. • talk when they're older.

____

____

____

____

____

____

____

SB pp. 86–87

A letter

1 WRITING A letter to the manager

Alyssa went to a rodeo with her family (pp. 64–65) and is now writing to the manager. Use the notes and the tips in the box to complete the letter.

- Alyssa Smith lives at 138 Peddlers Drive in Calgary AB T1X 3B4
- Writing to complain[1] about rodeo
- Reasons:
  - Time on poster was wrong: family got there an hour early
  - Family had to wait an hour to go in
  - No protection from the sun
  - Famous bronco rider Jack Spur didn't ride himself: his son rode
- Tickets weren't expensive
- Parents really enjoyed the rodeo

[1] **to complain** sich beschweren

Put Alyssa's name and address at the top of the page.

Canadians use the American or British way of writing the date.

Use the correct opening for a formal letter.

Paragraph 1: explain why Alyssa is writing.

Paragraph 2: give her opinion and reasons.

Paragraph 3: mention one or two good aspects about the day.

Closing: sum up or repeat her opinion.

Use a formal way to say goodbye.

You can find more help on SB pp. 88 and 161.

SB p. 88

Describing visuals

1 Facts about Canada

25 **a** LISTENING Listen to the speakers. Match each statement with the visual described. One visual is extra.

1		2		3		4	

A
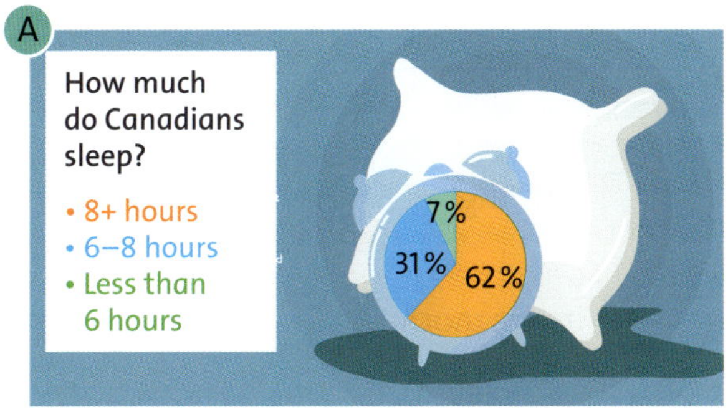

Source: General Social Survey, Time Use.

B Number of men per 100 women
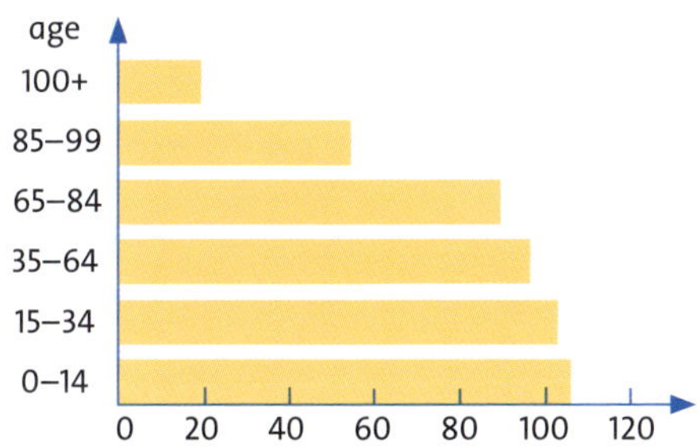

Source: Statistics Canada, Population Trends by Age and Sex, 2016 Census of Population.

E
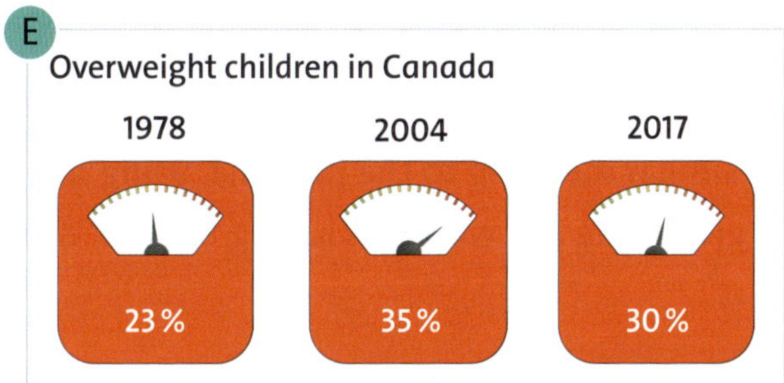

Source: Public Health Agency of Canada: Tackling Obesity in Canada.

C
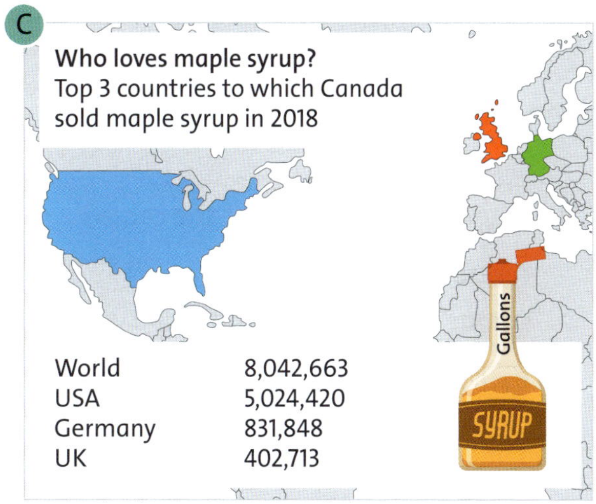

Source: Canadian International Merchandise Trade Database, Canada, Exports: Production and Value of Maple Products.

D Time-use survey: minutes per day

Country	Personal Care	paid work or study	unpaid work	Freetime activities	Other
Canada	637	305	186	279	34
Germany	648	248	196	331	17
United States	648	289	196	287	20

Source: OECD, Time Use.

b One visual from a is not described in the audio track. Write a description of it.

26 **c** LISTENING Listen to the conversation. Fill in the missing information.

d SPEAKING Partner A: Look at page 74. Partner B: Look at page 75.

Source: Ipsos, Canada Day: Some Fun Facts.

SB p. 89

I am still alive

1 READING Details from the text

a Look at the text SB pp. 90–91 and tick (✓) the right answers.

1 Which of these things does Jess take?
- ☐ a jar ☐ water ☐ food ☐ a knife

2 Why doesn't Jess want to go in the water?
- ☐ She can't swim. ☐ Bo can't swim. ☐ It's too cold. ☐ There's no boat.

3 What is Jess wearing on her feet?
- ☐ just shoes ☐ just socks ☐ nothing ☐ sandals

4 When does Jess arrive at the cabin?
- ☐ at night ☐ in the evening ☐ in the morning ☐ after two days

5 What kind of food doesn't Jess find in the cabin?
- ☐ rabbit ☐ carrots ☐ apples ☐ deer

b Find lines from the text that describe Jess's feelings. There may be more than one right answer.

1 impatient ____________________
2 hungry ____________________
3 careful ____________________
4 hurt ____________________
5 unsure ____________________
6 hopeful ____________________
7 worried ____________________
8 trusting ____________________
9 surprised ____________________
10 caring ____________________

SB pp. 90–91

2 New words, same meaning

Complete the second sentence so that it has a similar meaning to the first one, using the KEY WORD in brackets. Do not change the KEY WORD given. Use 2–5 words including the KEY WORD.

1 Everything else I leave by the cabin. (ALL)

I *leave all the other things* by the cabin.

2 I stare at the canoe, floating maybe twenty feet from the shore. (WHICH)

I stare at the canoe, ____________________ maybe twenty feet from the shore.

3 I whistle for Bo, but I don't wait for him. (WALK)

I whistle for Bo, but I start ____________________ him.

4 I have no idea where to turn off. (KNOW)

____________________ where to turn off.

5 It wouldn't be hard to miss the cabin in the woods. (EASY)

It ____________________ to miss the cabin in the woods.

6 It's a few minutes before I understand what this means. (AFTER)

____________________, I understand what this means.

SB pp. 90–91

1 Check your vocabulary

a What kind of visuals are these? Label each one.

1 ______________________

2 ______________________

3 ______________________

4 ______________________

5 ______________________

6 ______________________

7 ______________________

b Circle the word that doesn't go with the others on each line.

1 house	area	cabin	flat
2 fishing	exciting	hunting	hiking
3 canoeing	swimming	camping	diving
4 wilderness	woods	village	jungle
5 beach	shore	pool	lake
6 leaf	branch	fruit	grass
7 beaver	salmon	polar bear	marmot
8 plate	jar	glass	bottle

2 Check your language

a Fill in the missing words to make negative questions.

1 ____________ you buy tickets for the rodeo for tomorrow? → Yes, I did!

2 ____________ that cowgirl here last year? → Yes, she was.

3 ____________ the riders wear helmets? → Yes, they do.

4 ____________ they doing barrel jumping today? → No, they aren't.

5 ____________ you take part in the barrel race today? → Yes, I will.

b Complete each sentence with the correct emphatic pronoun.

1 Unfortunately, we didn't see any polar bears ________________.

2 I ________________ don't like snow very much, but my parents do!

3 She took these amazing photos ________________.

4 You ________________ nearly got attacked by a polar bear!

5 The polar bears ________________ don't want to meet people, but Churchill is in their path.

6 The prison ________________ is only one strategy for keeping the town safe from bears.

c Complete each sentence with the right form of *make* or *do*.

1 Our school ____________ a survey to find out what activities students would enjoy.

2 I haven't ____________ many friends in my new school yet.

3 She's been ____________ breakfast for the whole family every Sunday for years.

4 We don't have to ____________ any homework this weekend.

5 They haven't ____________ their chores yet today.

6 You have to ____________ a wish when you blow out the candles on your birthday cake!

3 Check your speaking

27

A new classmate is introducing himself to Olivier's class. Listen to what he says and complete the follow-up questions.

1 ____ last name?

2 ____ live in New Brunswick?

3 How many brothers and how many ______________________________?

4 Why did your family ______________________________?

5 ____ in a team in New Brunswick?

4 Check your writing

Ten words are missing or wrong in this letter. Underline each mistake and mark the places of missing words with an asterisk*. Then write the missing and correct word(s) on the right.

Dear Sir	____________
I write about an infographic that was published	____________
in your newspaper recently. It sayed that in the	____________
300,000 years that humans been on earth, we	____________
usselves have already threatened or killed more	____________
as a million kinds of plants and animals.	____________
After my opinion, this number is not right. It has	____________
really only taked us about 200 years to do this,	____________
since the start of earth warming.	____________
Yours faithful,	____________
Owen Johnson	

Unit 1

STUDY SKILLS exercise 2 | page 11

2 SPEAKING Around New York

a You and your partner are tourists in New York. Your partner describes three places she/he likes to visit to you. Tick (✓) the correct sights and tell her/him the name of each place.

- ☐ Grand Central Terminal
- ☐ a deli
- ☐ the Empire State Building
- ☐ the Statue of Liberty
- ☐ Times Square

b Now change roles. You want to go sightseeing, but can't remember the names of these places. Describe them to your partner. For example: It is a place where ... / You can do/see ... there.

SB p. 20

Unit 4

SKILLS TRAINING Speaking & Mediation exercise 2 | page 53

2 SPEAKING At the doctor's

You are a doctor. Put the lines of the dialogue in the right places. There are three extra lines. Then practise the dialogue with your partner.

What's the problem? • I'll check ... yes, your temperature is a little high. • What do you want? • Goodbye. • Stay at home and sleep as much as possible. • Hi, I'm Dr. Washington. What can I do for you? • Let me take a look. Yes, your throat looks red. • You're welcome. Get well soon! • No, you don't. Drink some tea with honey[1].

You: ____________________

Patient: I don't feel well. I'm coughing and I have a sore throat.

You: ____________________

Patient: I also have a temperature.

You: ____________________

Patient: Do I need antibiotics?

You: ____________________

Patient: What else can I do?

You: ____________________

Patient: OK, thank you!

You: ____________________

[1] **honey** Honig

SB p. 71

Unit 4

WORDS AND PICTURES exercise 2 | page 45

2 READING Short biographies

a **Read this short biography of Michelle Obama.**

Michelle Robinson Obama is a lawyer, writer, and the wife of the 44th President, Barack Obama. She was the first African American First Lady of the United States. She has become a role model for women, and works for education and in the field of health care.

Michelle Robinson grew up in a small house on the South Side of Chicago. Her father had a serious illness but almost never missed work. Her mother stayed at home to take care of Michelle and her brother.

After high school, Robinson went to Princeton University and then to Harvard Law School. She then worked as a lawyer in Chicago, where she later met Barack Obama. After a few years, Robinson stopped being a lawyer so she could help people in their neighbourhoods. The Obamas married in 1992 and later had two daughters, Sasha and Malia.

When her husband decided to try to become president, Michelle helped him. She travelled around the country and gave a lot of speeches. Barack's team said that Michelle's excellent speeches got many people to vote for her husband. Barack won in 2008.

As First Lady, she continued to try to help people. In 2010, she created a programme called *Let's Move!*, bringing together city leaders, parents, schools and people in health care to fight childhood obesity, which is the problem of children being overweight. In 2014, Obama started *Reach Higher*, a programme which helped young people continue their education past high school.

Since leaving the White House in 2017, Michelle Obama has mostly stayed out of the news. However, in 2018 she published her autobiography *Becoming*, which was very popular.

b **Circle the correct word/phrase to complete each sentence about Michelle Obama.**

1 Obama grew up without a *mother / father / sister.*

2 Obama's first job after university was: *a lawyer / First Lady / neighbourhood leader.*

3 Obama helped her husband become president by *travelling around the country / giving speeches / voting for him.*

4 Obama's programme *Let's Move!* works to prevent *fighting in school / obesity in children / childhood illnesses.*

5 Obama's career as a writer started *early /with problems / successfully.*

c **Make notes on Michelle Obama. Then give a one-minute talk about her to your partner.**

SB pp. 60–61

Unit 4

SKILLS TRAINING Speaking & Mediation exercise 2 | page 53

2 SPEAKING At the doctor's

You are at the doctor's. Put the lines of the dialogue in the right places. There are three extra lines. Then practise the dialogue with your partner.

OK, thank you! • What else can I do? • Do I need antibiotics? • I also have a temperature. • Help me! • I need antibiotics. • I don't feel well. I'm coughing and I have a sore throat. • What's the problem?

Doctor: Hi, I'm Dr. Washington. What can I do for you?

You: ______________________

Doctor: Let me take a look. Yes, your throat looks red.

You: ______________________

Doctor: I'll check ... yes, your temperature is a little high.

You: ______________________

Doctor: No, you don't. Drink some tea with honey[1].

You: ______________________

Doctor: Stay at home and sleep as much as possible.

You: ______________________

Doctor: You're welcome. Get well soon!

[1] **honey** Honig

SB p. 71

Unit 5

WORDS AND PICTURES exercise 2 | page 59

21

2 LISTENING AND SPEAKING Canada quiz

Test your partner on facts about Canada. Listen to Olivier, then ask the following questions and write down his/her answers. Then add up the points and give him/her a score. SB pp. 78–79

1 What are the two official languages of Canada? ______________________

2 When were parts of Canada colonized? ______________________

3 Quebec City is on how many rivers? ______________________

4 How many time zones does Canada have? ______________________

5 Where do most people in Canada live? ______________________

6 What per cent of people in Canada are from different countries? ______________________

Answers: **1** French and English • **2** in the sixteenth century • **3** two • **4** six • **5** near the border with the USA • **6** 20 %

Score: _____ points	**1–3 points** Listen again! • **4–5 points** Good listening skills! • **6 points** Expert!

Unit 5

WORDS AND PICTURES exercise 2 | page 59

21

2 LISTENING AND SPEAKING Canada quiz

Test your partner on facts about Canada. Listen to Olivier, then ask the following questions and write down his/her answers. Then add up the points and give him/her a score. SB pp. 78–79

1 Which countries colonized parts of Canada? ____________

2 Who is the head of state of Canada? ____________

3 Name three sports that are popular in Canada. ____________

4 Which country is bigger than Canada? ____________

5 How many people live in Canada? ____________

6 Name three kinds of wild animals that live in Canada. ____________

Answers: **1** France and Britain • **2** the British king or queen • **3** ice hockey, lacrosse and basketball • **4** Russia • **5** 36 million • **6** *e.g.*: bears, beavers, moose, polar bears, salmon, whales, wolves

Score: ______ points	**1–3 points** Listen again! • **4–5 points** Good listening skills! • **6 points** Expert!

Unit 5

STUDY SKILLS exercise 1 | page 67

1 Facts about Canada

d SPEAKING Look at the infographic. Take turns to ask or answer questions to fill in the gaps. The words and phrases on SB p. 89 can help you. SB pp. 89

Young Canadians ...

are social
48% of them ____________ and 71% give to ____________.
________ belong to a group or organization.

face challenges
17% of young people have been ____________ in the last five years.

are educated
about ________ of young men and ________ of young women had a college degree in 2017.

use technology
almost ________ of them use the internet daily or have their own smartphone. 93% of these young people use social networking sites.

Source: Statistics Canada. A Portrait of Canadian Youth.

Unit 5

STUDY SKILLS exercise 1 | page 67

1 Facts about Canada

d SPEAKING Look at the infographic. Take turns to ask or answer questions to fill in the gaps. The words and phrases on SB p. 89 can help you.

SB pp. 89

Young Canadians …

are social
______ of them volunteer and ______ give to charities. 67% belong to a ______ or ______.

face challenges
______ of young people have been cyberbullied in the last five years.

are educated
about 52% of young men and 70% of young women had a ______ degree in ______.

use technology
almost 100% of them use the internet daily or have their own ______.
93% of these young people use social networking sites.

Source: Statistics Canada. A Portrait of Canadian Youth.

Revision 2

exercise 3 | page 58

3 A crazy weekend

a Ask your partner to give you words to fill each gap to make a silly story.

After ______ (a/an + adjective) day with ______ (name of a friend) on Saturday, I was really looking forward to ______ (a/an + adjective) day on Sunday. After my ______ (adjective to describe a food) breakfast of ______ (a food), I put on my favourite ______ (colour) ______ (piece of clothing) and went out with my ______ (family member). We got in our ______ (type of vehicle) to go to ______ (city). There was a lot of traffic, so it took us ______ (number) hours. We wanted to ______ (infinitive verb) there, but we couldn't get tickets. We decided to go ______ (*ing*-form of verb) instead. That was really fun, especially the part where we got to try ______ (*ing*-form of verb) for the first time! I hope we can do it again next ______ (day or month).

b Read the text to the class.

Unit 1 p. 13, p. 14

1 Check your vocabulary

a There are a lot of ways to get around the five *boroughs* of New York. For example, you can take one of 27 subway *lines/routes* or hail a *taxi*. There's usually a lot of *traffic* in New York, so taxis can be quite slow! When you arrive, the driver will tell you the *fare*. Give a *tip* of about 15–20 %.
If you're staying at a hotel, you will check *in* with the receptionist. Make sure to get a *key* card for each person in your room. Don't forget: what Americans call the *first* floor is the ground floor in the UK.

b

vending	an application	1	*vending machine*
state of	date	2	*state of mind*
homeless	insurance	3	*homeless shelter*
health	machine	4	*health insurance*
fill in	mind	5	*fill in an application*
expiration	shelter	6	*expiration date*

2 Check your language

1	*Where are you from?*	I'm from Rome, Italy.
2	*Is this your first time in New York?*	Yes, it's my first time in New York.
3	*How long are you staying in New York?*	I'm staying for one week.
4	*Why did you come to New York?*	Because I wanted to visit the places I have seen in movies.
5	*Do you like New York / it here?*	Yes, I think New York is amazing!
6	*What room are you (staying) in?*	I'm in room 891.
7	*Who is that?*	Oh, that's my mother.
8	*Where are you going / What are you doing today?*	We're going to the Empire State Building this morning and to the American Museum of Natural History in the afternoon.

3 Check your listening and speaking

a

Receptionist:	Welcome to the Midnight Manhattan Hotel. How can I help you?	*Can I help you?*
Zara:	Yes, please. We've booked a room for three nights.	*We've booked a room for four nights.*
Receptionist:	What's the name of the person who booked the room?	*Can you please give me the name of the person who booked the room?*
Zara:	Zara Elliott. That's me.	
Receptionist:	Ah, yes, Ms Elliot. So here's your key card. It's room 318 on the 3rd floor.	
Jordan:	Can we have two key cards?	*May we have two key cards, please?*
Receptionist:	No problem. Here you are.	*Of course.*
Zara:	Where's the elevator?	*Where can we find the elevator?*

Receptionist: It's over there, on the right. — *It's over there, on the left.*
Jordan: Oh, I see it. Thank you.
Zara: When is checkout? — *What time is checkout?*
Receptionist: You have to leave the room by 11:00 am.
Jordan: OK, thank you.

4 Check your writing

Applicant Information			
Name: *Zara*	*Elliott*	*Date* of Birth:	*5/19/2000*
First Name	*Family* Name	Gender: ◎ *Male*	☒ *Female*
Are you a *citizen* of the United States?		◎ YES	☒ NO
If not, *country* of citizenship?		*England*	
Passport Number? *09829571093*			
Issue Date: *3/4/2020*		*Expiration* Date:	*3/4/2030*

Unit 2 p. 27, p. 28

1 Check your vocabulary

a

Native Americans are the *indigenous* people of the United States. Many *stereotypes* about Native Americans are not true. For example, only about a third live on *reservations*. Most Native Americans don't wear traditional dress every day, although many wear their hair in *braids*. A headdress made of *feathers* is a sacred thing worn by some tribes, especially by the tribal *elders*. These are older tribe *members* who know a lot about the traditions and culture of the tribe and give advice to others.

b

drop out of school

driving licence

quotation marks

break down

gun control

health care

2 Check your language

a
1. Emma González *would like* it if the United States *banned* guns.
2. It's hard to *do* online research if you *don't have* a computer at home.
3. Grace *will spread* more awareness, if she *gives* more presentations about the Kewa pueblo across the country.
4. The Choctaw boy's mother thought that if the family *took* blankets from the soldiers, they *would/could/might get* sick.

b
1. She didn't prepare *herself* for this debate topic at all!
2. You need to listen to *each other* carefully during a debate.
3. I'm not very good at expressing *myself* when debating this topic.
4. The other team hurt *itself* in the debate with that silly argument.
5. I'd like you all to help *each other* prepare for the debate.

3 Check your mediation skills

1. *I really liked the film/movie.*
2. *I thought the camerawork was great, especially the close-ups.*
3. *How did you like the last scene?*
4. *I don't agree (with that/you).*
5. *Why would you recommend this film/movie to others?*

4 Check your speaking

a Good *morning/afternoon* everyone! Today I'm going to *talk about* the film *Dances with Wolves*. *Firstly*, I'm going to tell you about the plot. *Secondly*, I'll *discuss* if Native Americans are shown realistically in the film. *Thirdly*, I'll give my personal *opinion* of the film.
In the film, which takes place during the Civil War a soldier named John Dunbar hurts his leg very badly, so a doctor wants to cut it off. Here you *can see* a photo of Dunbar from the film. The soldier doesn't want to live with one leg and tries to commit *suicide*. He doesn't die and a better doctor saves his leg. Dunbar asks to go to the West, where he meets a *tribe* of Lakota Native *Americans*. He decides to leave his old life to live with them. They give him the name Dances with Wolves. He falls in love with a white woman who also lives with the tribe. ...

Unit 3 p. 41, p. 42

1 Check your vocabulary

a Radio DJs wear *headphones* on their ears and talk into a *microphone*. Radio *stations* don't just play music – they also report the news and play adverts and public service *announcements*. The music on the radio is *recorded* in a studio.

b

Word	Definition
1 to repair	*to make something whole or able to work again*
2 *necessary*	so important that you must do or have it

3 cotton	*a plant that is used to make cloth*
4 pocket	*a small piece of cloth, like a small bag, in or on clothes*
5 *zipper*	a thing with teeth that you use to close bags
6 salmon	*a large silver fish that lives in Alaska*

2 Check your language

a
1. After seeing a bookcase on the pavement, I called my friend and we carried it to my house.
   After I saw a bookcase on the pavement, …
2. Wanting to recycle a glass bottle, I put some pretty Christmas lights in it.
   Because I wanted to recycle a glass bottle, …
3. Taking a small stick, we put little pieces of old newspapers around it to make flowers.
   We took/take a small stick and …
4. Using a knife, I carefully cut around the plastic bottle.
   I used a knife and …

b Before fridges **(1)** *were invented*, iceboxes **(2)** *were used* to keep food cold. Ice **(3)** *was taken* to people's houses by a horse and wagon. Iceboxes **(4)** *were made* of wood, with metal on the inside walls. Food **(5)** *was kept* cold inside by the ice.
Today, of course, our food **(6)** *is cooled* by modern fridges that use electricity. Instead of ice, frozen food **(7)** *is transported* to many people's houses.

3 Check your listening

1 Alaska is the … state of the US.	*49th*
2 Lake Clark is one of the … national parks in the US.	*largest*
3 The park protects landscapes, … and people.	*wildlife*
4 Lake Clark isn't … by many natural disasters.	*threatened*
5 Lightning has caused … in the park.	*wildfires*
6 It is very … to get to the park.	*difficult*
7 Brad and Cindy Levine like the park because it isn't very …	*crowded*
8 They are most interested in seeing …	*bears*
9 There is a large population of red … in the park.	*salmon*

4 Check your writing

Big disapointment ★★★☆☆

I have to say that I'm really disappointed with the video game *Underground Life 6*. The only reason I'm giving it three stars is because the graphics are very **(1)** latest / realistic. The world is very **(2)** big / proper and a lot of fun to discover. **(3)** But / Therefore as **(4)** beautiful / virtual as it looks, there are a lot of problems with this game.

Firstly, this isn't like the other *Underground Life* games. The beginning of the game is **(5)** easy / hard to understand and leaves too much information out. You have to play a lot of short games that are all very **(6)** similar / organic to get to the next level.

(7) In addition / Although, you really have to buy **(8)** extra / sustainable weapons. **(9)** And / So if you don't buy them, you're not **(10)** tall / strong enough to win fights.

Secondly, the game didn't always work with my system. A few times I had to start the game over. Sometimes **(11)** new / difficult characters suddenly appear and then quickly disappear. I hope they repair the problems soon!

Thirdly, **(12)** although / because the graphics are **(13)** great / colourful, the sound is **(14)** tasty / terrible! Without headphones, I couldn't understand what the characters were saying. And the background music is really **(15)** annoyed / annoying.

(16) Overall / However, I can't recommend this game. Try one of the other *Underground Life* games instead – they're a lot better!

Unit 4 p. 55, p. 56

1 Check your vocabulary

a
1 segregation — *different seats on buses for blacks and whites*
2 civil war — *in the US in the 1800s between north and south*
3 victim — *Freddie Gray / Trayvon Martin / Tamir Rice / ...*
4 trial — *George Zimmerman's trial because he shot Trayvon Martin*
5 scrapbook — *Kelisha's scrapbook about African American role models*
6 sportsperson — *Simone Biles / Muhammad Ali / Colin Kaepernick / ...*
7 seafood — *oyster/crab/fish*
8 vehicle — *the Dominator / (police) car / train ...*

b
1 When he's talking to Starr, Khalil calls the police officer a *fool*.
2 The police officer points his *flashlight* at Khalil to see his face.
3 He asks for *proof* of Khalil's insurance.
4 Khalil gets the documents out of his *wallet*.
5 Starr remembers the police officer's *badge* number.
6 The police officer wears his hair in a *buzz* cut.
7 One-Fifteen has a *scar* over his *lip*.
8 The police officer wants Starr to put her hands on the *dashboard*.
9 Khalil *gasps* after he's shot the second time.

2 Check your language

a
1 She threw me the beads. *She threw the beads to me*.
2 He gave her a costume. *He gave a costume to her*.

b
1 I brought a po' boy to her. *I brought her a po' boy*.
2 We sent a king cake to them. *We sent them a king cake*.

c
1 If I hadn't eaten the seafood, *I wouldn't have got sick*.
2 She wouldn't have won a gold medal *if she hadn't practised/trained hard*.
3 The law would never have been changed *if people hadn't protested*.

3 Check your mediation skills

1 Am Telefon fragst du, ob der Arzt morgen noch einen freien Termin hat.
Can I get an appointment for tomorrow, please?

2 Du sagst, dass du gegen Hunde allergisch bist.
I'm allergic to dogs.

3 Du fragst den Arzt, ob du Antibiotika brauchst.
Do I need antibiotics?

4 Check your writing

Serena Williams

In addition to being won of the greatest tennisplayers ever, Serena Williams is a big supporter of the Black Lives Matter moment. She was one of the first famous sportsperson to speak out about the killing of teenager Michael Brown. He has told other aktivists not to give up. Williams has also speaked about being worried that boys in her family could be victims from police shootings. She's not afraid to say what she thought!
Williams has winned more Grand Slam competitions then any other woman or man! Her sister Venus is also a grate player and they've won lots of game together.

one
tennis players
movement
sportspeople
She
activists, spoken/talked
of
thinks
won
than
great
games

Unit 5 p. 69, p. 70

1 Check your vocabulary

a
1 *infographic*
2 *line chart*
3 *map*
4 *Venn diagram*
5 *table*
6 *pie chart*
7 *bar chart*

1
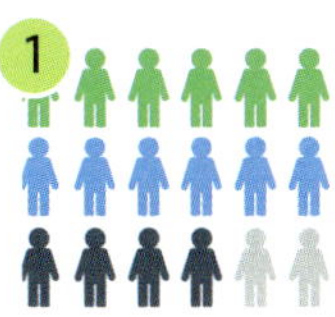

2

3
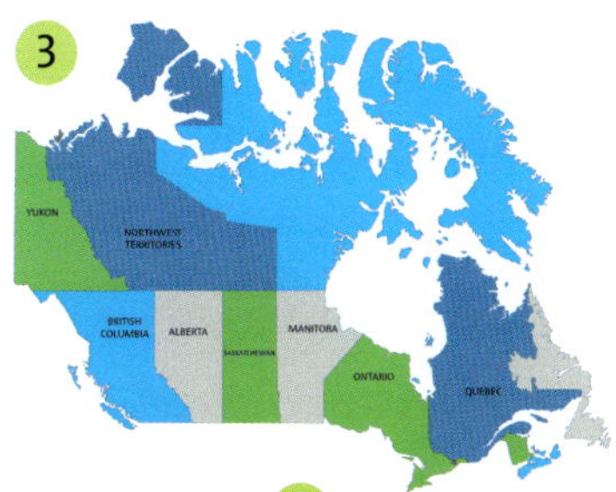

4
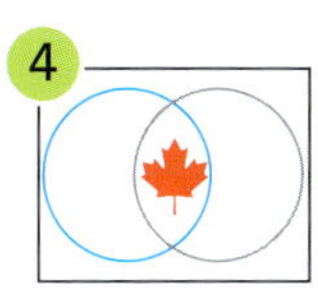

5

ROUP H	GAMES			
Country	P	W	L	%
Canada	0	0	0	0
Senegal	0	0	0	0
Lithuania	0	0	0	0
Australia	0	0	0	0

6
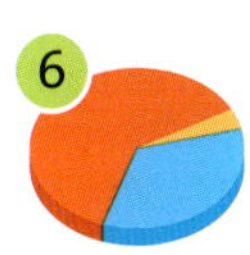

7
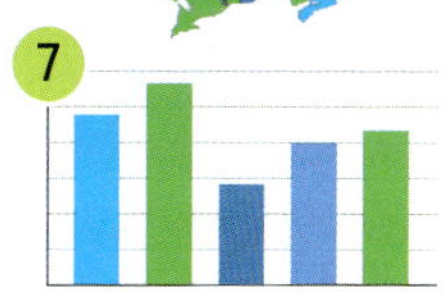

b

1	house	**(area)**	cabin	flat
2	fishing	**(exciting)**	hunting	hiking
3	canoeing	swimming	**(camping)**	diving
4	wilderness	woods	**(village)**	jungle
5	beach	shore	**(pool)**	lake
6	leaf	branch	fruit	**(grass)**
7	beaver	**(salmon)**	polar bear	marmot
8	**(plate)**	jar	glass	bottle

2 Check your language

a
1. *Didn't* you buy tickets for the rodeo for tomorrow? → Yes, I did!
2. *Wasn't* that cowgirl here last year? → Yes, she was.
3. *Don't* the riders wear helmets? → Yes, they do.
4. *Aren't* they doing barrel jumping today? → No, they aren't.
5. *Won't* you take part in the barrel race today? → Yes, I will.

b
1. Unfortunately, we didn't see any polar bears *ourselves*.
2. I *myself* don't like snow very much, but my parents do!
3. She took these amazing photos *herself*.
4. You *yourself/yourselves* nearly got attacked by a polar bear!
5. The polar bears *themselves* don't want to meet people, but Churchill is in their path.
6. The prison *itself* is only one strategy for keeping the town safe from bears.

c
1. Our school *does/did* a survey to find out what activities students would enjoy.
2. I haven't *made* many friends in my new school yet.
3. She's been *making* breakfast for the whole family every Sunday for years.
4. We don't have to *do* any homework this weekend.
5. They haven't *done* their chores yet today.
6. You have to *make* a wish when you blow out the candles on your birthday cake!

3 Check your speaking

1. *What's / What is your* last name?
2. *Where did you / For how long did you* live in New Brunswick?
3. How many brothers and how many *sisters do you have*?
4. Why did your family *move to Quebec / leave New Brunswick*?
5. *Did you play (ice hockey)* in a team in New Brunswick?

4 Check your writing

Dear Sir*	*or Madam,*
I write about an infographic that was published	*am writing*
in your newspaper recently. It sayed that in the	*said*
300,000 years that humans*been on earth, we	*have*
usselves have already threatened or killed more	*ourselves*
as a million kinds of plants and animals.	*than*
After my opinion, this number is not right. It has	*In*
really only taked us about 200 years to do this,	*taken*
since the start of earth warming.	*global*
Yours faithful,	*faithfully*
Owen Johnson	

REVISION 1 p. 29, p. 30

1 Describing people • Clothes • In a shop

Simple present

The store sells a lot of cool clothes. (There are nice hats and sunglasses on the shelves. The shoes are expensive. I can see a girl with curly hair, an overweight man with his son and an older woman and a tall man with glasses at the counter.)

Present progressive

The woman at the counter is buying a blue jacket. (The tall man is working at the counter. The girl is wearing a green dress and looking at herself in the mirror. The boy is trying on a pair of shoes.)

2 Parts of the body • Health

Ed: Hi Taylor! **(1)** *Have you been waiting* here long?
Taylor: I **(2)** *'ve/have been* here for about 20 minutes.
Ed: Aren't you feeling well?
Taylor: No, my stomach **(3)** *has been hurting* all day. What's wrong with you?
Ed: I **(4)** *'ve/have had* a sore throat since yesterday. But it's worse now.
Taylor: **(5)** *Have you been drinking* enough?
Ed: Yes ..., I **(6)** *'ve/have filled* my bottle three times today.
Nurse: Taylor Davis, that's the second time I **(7)** *'ve/have called* your name!
Taylor: Sorry! I **(8)** *'ve/have been talking* to Ed and I didn't hear you!

3 Places in the city • Asking for directions

a
1. *Could you tell me the way to 5th Avenue?*
2. *Which route should we take to Queens?*
3. *Have you ever been to a Broadway show?*
4. *How do we get to the museum?*
5. *How many blocks is it to the hotel?*
6. *Do you want to go to Ellis Island?*

b *(What is the sight called? / What can you do/see there? / How do we get to the sight? / Where is the sight?)*

c *American Museum of Natural History*

d

4 Booking a room

		true	false
1	Alison doesn't want to book online.	☐	☑
2	Alison wants to stay for five nights.	☑	☐
3	Only deluxe rooms are still free.	☐	☑
4	All the rooms have a bathtub.	☐	☑
5	The receptionist is friendly.	☑	☐
6	Alison books a standard room.	☐	☑

REVISION 2 p. 57, p. 58

1 Chores

1 Sergio and Sara *were walking* the dog when they *met* Emily.
2 Sara *was vacuuming* the floor when she *found* a pound coin.
3 Sergio *was doing* the dishes when he *broke* a glass.
4 Sofia *locked* herself out of the house while she *was taking out* the trash.
5 While Símon *was setting* the table, his father *burnt* the dinner.
6 It *started* to rain while Sofia *was mowing* the grass.

2 Holidays

a

Hi Neve!
I'm having the *great* / *greatest* holiday! Today we went to the *most cool* / *coolest* water park I've ever seen. The slides were even *longer* / *longest* than the ones at AquaFunLand … but also a little *more dangerous* / *dangerouser*. The water wasn't *as* / *so* warm as in AquaFunLand, but it was definitely *cleaner* / *more clean*. They had four diving boards: the *most low* / *lowest* one was just a one-metre board, but they had a high one that was three metres and a *higher* / *more high* one that was five metres. The *most high* / *highest* one was ten metres!
Tomorrow we're going to a museum. I think it will be a little less exciting *as* / *than* the water park.
See you soon!
Rana

b
1 If we *had known* you were going there, we could have gone together!
2 If you *have* some photos of the park, please send them to me!
3 We *will book* a room if the hotel isn't full.
4 We would stay in the hotel's best room if we *had* enough money.
5 The website says that the park *is* cheaper if you go in the winter.
6 If my mother's boss let her take a holiday, she *would/could/might come* too.
7 My sister gets an ear infection if she *stays* in the water too long.
8 I *would have written* to you yesterday if I hadn't been so tired.

3 A crazy weekend

Individuelle Lösungen

Tense overview

Aktiv			
Zeiten	**Formen**	**Bildung**	**Deutsch**
Present			
simple	*I play, he plays*	Infinitiv (+ *-s/-es* bei *he/she/it*)	ich spiele, er spielt
progressive	*I am playing*	Form von *be* + Infinitiv + *ing*	ich spiele gerade
Past			
simple	*I played*	Infinitiv + *-ed*	ich spielte
progressive	*I was playing*	Vergangenheit von *be* + Infinitiv + *ing*	ich spielte gerade
Present perfect			
simple	*I have played*	*have/has* + 3. Form des Verbs	ich habe gespielt
progressive	*I have been playing*	*have/has been* + Infinitiv + *ing*	ich habe gerade gespielt/ ich spiele schon seit ...
Past perfect			
simple	*I had played*	*had* + 3. Form des Verbs	ich hatte gespielt
Future			
will	*I will play*	will + Infinitiv	ich werde spielen
going to	*I am going to play*	Form von *be* + *going to* + Infinitiv	ich werde spielen

Passiv			
Zeiten	**Formen**	**Bildung**	**Deutsch**
Present			
simple	*I am asked*	Form von *be* + 3. Form des Verbs	ich werde gefragt
Past			
simple	*I was asked*	Vergangenheit von *be* + 3. Form des Verbs	ich wurde gefragt

Irregular verbs

infinitive	simple past	past participle	*Bedeutung*
(to) **be**	I/he/she/it **was**; you/we/you/they **were**	**been**	sein
(to) **beat**	**beat**	**beaten**	schlagen, besiegen
(to) **become**	**became**	**become**	werden
(to) **begin**	**began**	**begun**	anfangen, beginnen
°(to) **bite** [aɪ]	**bit** [ɪ]	**bitten** [ɪ]	beißen
(to) **bleed**	**bled**	**bled**	bluten
(to) **blow**	**blew** [uː]	**blown**	pusten, blasen; wehen
(to) **break** [eɪ]	**broke**	**broken**	brechen
(to) **bring**	**brought**	**brought**	bringen, mitbringen
(to) **build** [ɪ]	**built** [ɪ]	**built** [ɪ]	bauen
(to) **burn**	**burnt**	**burnt**	brennen, verbrennen
(to) **buy**	**bought**	**bought**	kaufen
(to) **catch**	**caught**	**caught**	(ein)fangen; erwischen
(to) **choose**	**chose**	**chosen**	wählen, auswählen
(to) **come**	**came**	**come**	kommen

infinitive	simple past	past participle	*Bedeutung*
(to) **cost**	**cost**	**cost**	kosten
(to) **cut**	**cut**	**cut**	schneiden; *(Rasen)* mähen
(to) **do**	**did**	**done** [ʌ]	tun, machen
(to) **dig**	**dug**	**dug**	graben
(to) **draw**	**drew**	**drawn**	zeichnen
(to) **drink**	**drank**	**drunk**	trinken
(to) **drive** [aɪ]	**drove** [əʊ]	**driven** [ɪ]	fahren
(to) **eat** [iː]	**ate** [et, eɪt]	**eaten** [iː]	essen
(to) **fall**	**fell**	**fallen**	fallen
(to) **feed**	**fed**	**fed**	füttern
(to) **feel**	**felt**	**felt**	fühlen, sich fühlen
(to) **fight**	**fought**	**fought**	kämpfen, bekämpfen
(to) **find**	**found**	**found**	finden
(to) **fly**	**flew**	**flown**	fliegen
(to) **forget**	**forgot**	**forgotten**	vergessen
(to) **freeze**	**froze**	**frozen**	(ge)frieren; erstarren
(to) **get**	**got**	**got**	bekommen; (sich etw.) besorgen, holen
(to) **give** [ɪ]	**gave**	**given** [ɪ]	geben
(to) **go**	**went**	**gone**	gehen, fahren
(to) **grow**	**grew**	**grown**	anbauen; werden; wachsen
(to) **hang**	**hung** [ʌ]	**hung**	hängen
(to) **have**	**had**	**had**	haben
(to) **hear** [ɪə]	**heard** [ɜː]	**heard**	hören
(to) **hide**	**hid**	**hidden**	(sich) verstecken
(to) **hit**	**hit**	**hit**	treffen auf, schlagen, prallen, stoßen
(to) **hold**	**held**	**held**	halten
(to) **hurt**	**hurt**	**hurt**	verletzen; wehtun
(to) **keep**	**kept**	**kept**	(be)halten
(to) **kneel**	**knelt**	**knelt**	knien
(to) **know** [nəʊ]	**knew** [njuː]	**known** [nəʊn]	wissen; kennen
(to) **lead**	**led**	**led**	führen, leiten
(to) **leave**	**left**	**left**	lassen, zurücklassen, verlassen
(to) **lend**	**lent**	**lent**	(ver)leihen
(to) **let**	**let**	**let**	lassen
(to) **lose** [uː]	**lost**	**lost**	verlieren
(to) **make**	**made**	**made**	machen, herstellen
(to) **mean** [iː]	**meant** [e]	**meant** [e]	bedeuten; sagen wollen
(to) **meet**	**met**	**met**	treffen
(to) **pay**	**paid**	**paid**	(be)zahlen
(to) **put**	**put**	**put**	legen, stellen, stecken
(to) **read** [iː]	**read** [e]	**read** [e]	lesen
(to) **ride** [aɪ]	**rode**	**ridden** [ɪ]	reiten; *(Rad)* fahren

infinitive	simple past	past participle	*Bedeutung*
(to) **ring**	**rang**	**rung**	läuten, klingeln
(to) **rise**	**rose**	**risen**	(an)steigen; sich erheben
(to) **run**	**ran**	**run**	rennen, laufen
(to) **say**	**said** [sed]	**said** [sed]	sagen
(to) **see**	**saw**	**seen**	sehen
(to) **sell**	**sold**	**sold**	verkaufen
(to) **send**	**sent**	**sent**	senden, schicken
(to) **set**	**set**	**set**	stellen, legen, setzen
(to) **sew**	**sewed**	**sewn**	nähen
(to) **shake**	**shook**	**shaken**	schütteln
(to) **shoot**	**shot**	**shot**	(er)schießen
(to) **show**	**showed**	**shown**	zeigen
(to) **sing**	**sang**	**sung**	singen
(to) **sit**	**sat**	**sat**	sitzen; sich setzen
(to) **sleep**	**slept**	**slept**	schlafen
(to) **speak** [iː]	**spoke**	**spoken**	sprechen
(to) **speed**	**sped**	**sped**	rasen, zu schnell fahren
(to) **spend**	**spent**	**spent**	*(Geld)* ausgeben, *(Zeit)* verbringen
(to) **spin**	**spun**	**spun**	(sich) drehen
(to) **spread**	**spread**	**spread**	verbreiten, sich ausbreiten
(to) **stand**	**stood**	**stood**	stehen
(to) **steal**	**stole**	**stolen**	stehlen, rauben
°(to) **stick**	**stuck**	**stuck**	kleben
(to) **swim**	**swam**	**swum**	schwimmen
(to) **take**	**took**	**taken**	(mit)nehmen; bringen
(to) **teach** [iː]	**taught** [ɔː]	**taught** [ɔː]	lehren, unterrichten
(to) **tell**	**told**	**told**	sagen; erzählen, berichten
(to) **think**	**thought**	**thought**	denken, glauben, meinen
(to) **throw**	**threw**	**thrown**	werfen
(to) **understand**	**understood**	**understood**	verstehen
(to) **wake up**	**woke up**	**woken up**	aufwachen; (auf)wecken
(to) **wear** [eə]	**wore** [ɔː]	**worn** [ɔː]	tragen *(Kleidung)*
(to) **win**	**won** [ʌ]	**won** [ʌ]	gewinnen
(to) **write** [aɪ]	**wrote**	**written** [ɪ]	schreiben

°Mit diesem Kringel sind Wörter markiert, die nicht zum Lernwortschatz gehören.

Quellenverzeichnis

Titelbild: Shutterstock GmbH (Läufer: Maridav; Brooklyn Bridge, NYC: Andrey Bayda)

Illustrationen:

Christian Bartz: **S. 29**; **S. 32**; **S. 37**; **S. 57**; **S. 64**; **S. 65**
Carlos Borrell Eiköter: **S. 30** u.; **S. 83**

Fotos:

S. 3: Shutterstock.com/S. Borisov; **S. 5** o.: Shutterstock.com/robert paul van beets; u.: Shutterstock.com/littlenySTOCK; **S. 6**: Shutterstock.com/Nathan Kresge; **S. 7:** Cornelsen/designcollective – eberhard & thron GbR/Petra Eberhard; 2: U.S. Department of Homeland Security, 2019. **S. 9**: Shutterstock.com/Jon Bilous; **S. 10** o. re.: Bridgeman Images/Buyenlarge Archive//UIG; o. li.: Shutterstock.com/Monkey Business Images; Äpfel: Shutterstock.com/Eva Speshneva; elevator: Shutterstock.com/Smach2003; movie theater: Shutterstock.com/Syda Productions; subway: Shutterstock.com/Olga Listopad; sneakers: Shutterstock.com/Roman Samokhin; cell phone: Shutterstock.com/Oleksiy Mark; restroom: Shutterstock.com/Kostsov; **S. 11** o.: dpa Picture-Alliance/Klaus Nowottn; Mi. li.: Shutterstock.com/f11photo; Mi. Mi.: Shutterstock.com/Monkey Business Images; Mi. re.: mauritius Images/alamy stock photo/NYCPW Photography; u.: World Trade Center: Shutterstock.com/otherstock; Bronx Zoo: Shutterstock.com/Elizaveta Galitckaia; Statue of Liberty: Shutterstock.com/RodClementPhotography; Brooklyn Bridge: Shutterstock.com/Benedikt Juerges; Central Park: Shutterstock.com/GagliardiPhotography; **S. 12**: Shutterstock.com/Gordana Sermek; **S. 16** (1): Shutterstock.com/Matej Kastelic; (2): mauritius images/alamy stock photo/Patti McConville; (3): mauritius images/Hemis.fr; (4): Shutterstock.com/Dmitrijs Dmitrijevs; (5): mauritius images/alamy stock photo/Len Holsborg; (6): Shutterstock.com/Yulia Mayorova; (7): mauritius images/Cavan Images; (8): Shutterstock.com/GagliardiPhotography; (9): Shutterstock.com/Maridav; (10): Shutterstock.com/oneinchpunch; **S. 17** u. v. li. n. re (1) (Ausschnitt): Shutterstock.com/Stockshakir; (2): Shutterstock.com/c12; (3): Shutterstock.com/Melanina Evgeniya; (4): Shutterstock.com/The Clay Machine Gun; (5): Shutterstock.com/Bogdan Denysyuk; **S. 18** Party Hut: Shutterstock.com/Yayayoyo; Tüte: Shutterstock.com/TyBy; Buch: Shutterstock.com/mayrum; Kamera: Shutterstock.com/karnoff; **S. 19** v. o. li. n. u. re (1): Shutterstock.com/Eric Isselee; (2): Shutterstock.com/sirtravelalot; (3): Shutterstock.com/Zurijeta; (4): Shutterstock.com/AlonaP; (5): Shutterstock.com/Lightspring; (6): Shutterstock.com/Frenchwildlifephotograher; **S. 22**: Shutterstock.com/Goodreason; **S. 23**: Shutterstock.com/Lightspring; **S. 24**: Shutterstock.com/fizkes; **S. 25** o.: Imago Stock & People GmbH/ZUMA Press/Kristin Callahan; u. (Ausschnitt): Imago Stock & People GmbH/MediaPunch/Faye Sadou; **S. 27** v. li. n. re (1): Shutterstock.com/igor kisselev; (2): Shutterstock.com/grapop; (3): Shutterstock.com/Jon Bilous; (4): Shutterstock.com/Irina Strelnikova; (5): Shutterstock.com/DeiMosz; (6): Shutterstock.com/Maxx-Studio; **S. 30** o.: mauritius images/alamy stock photo/Patti McConville; Männchen in der Karte (Ausschnitt): Shutterstock.com/Bardocz Peter; **S. 31** factory: Shutterstock.com/Vyntage Visuals; wolves: Shutterstock.com/creativex; volunteers: Shutterstock.com/ESB Professional; music: Shutterstock.com/DisobeyArt; **S. 33**: Shutterstock.com/Siberian Art; **S. 34** o.: Shutterstock.com/Syda Productions; Icons Mi: Shutterstock.com/KerdaZz; **S. 36**: Shutterstock.com/pikepicture; **S. 38**: Shutterstock.com/Maximilia; **S. 39** o. li.: Shutterstock.com/Rvector; o. re.: Shutterstock.com/Macrovector; **S. 42**: Shutterstock.com/Michael J Thompson; **S. 43** (1): Shutterstock.com/PHIL LENOIR; (2): Shutterstock.com/chyworks; (3): Shutterstock.com/WhitePlaid; (4): Shutterstock.com/Rtstudio; **S. 47**: Mural of Freddie Gray by Street art artist Nether and Brandon Ross, Baltimore 2015: Imago Stock & People GmbH/ZUMA Press; **S. 48**: Imago Sportfotodienst GmbH/ZUMA Press; **S. 49** a: Shutterstock.com/CaseyMartin; b: Shutterstock.com/cvalle; c: Shutterstock.com/Joyce Marrero; d: Shutterstock.com/hlphoto; e: akg-images/UIG/Universal History Archive; f: mauritius images/alamy stock photo/eddie linssen; **S. 50**: dpa Picture-Alliance/ASSOCIATED PRESS/Alex Brandon/Ausschnitt: CSV; **S. 52**: Centers for Disease Control and Prevention: Be Ready! Tornados, 2019; **S. 53**: Shutterstock.com/Lisa F. Young; **S. 54**: Imago Stock & People GmbH/Matrix; **S. 56**: Imago Stock & People GmbH/PA Images/Doug Peters; **S. 58**: Shutterstock.com/Pressmaster; **S. 59** (1): Shutterstock.com/Darryl Brooks; (2): Shutterstock.com/Lester Balajadia; (3): Shutterstock.com/Rawpixel.com; (4): mauritius images/alamy stock photo/The Picture Art Collection; (5): Shutterstock.com/curiosity; loon: Shutterstock.com/Brian Lasenby; **S. 61**: Shutterstock.com/FloridaStock; **S. 62**: Shutterstock.com/Olesia Bilkei; **S. 63**: Shutterstock.com/farbled; **S. 67** A: Shutterstock.com/practicuum; Statistik: General Social Survey, Time Use, 2015.; B: Statistik: Statistics Canada: Population Trends by Age and Sex, 2016 Census of Population, 2017.; C: Shutterstock.com/Volina; Syrup: Shutterstock.com/grmarc; Statistik: Canadian International Merchandise Trade Database, Canada, Exports: Production and Value of Maple Products, 2018. ; D: Statistik: Organisation for Economic co-operation and Development (OECD): Time Use, 2015.; E: Shutterstock.com/Kyryloff; Statistik: Public Health Agency of Canada: Tackling Obesity in Canada, 2019.; u. re. Hintergrund: Shutterstock.com/Dmytro Balkhovitin; Ahornblatt: Shutterstock.com/Lightspring; Statistik: Ipsos, Canada Day: Some Fun Facts, 2015.; **S. 69**: (1,3 und 7) Ausschnitte: Shutterstock.com/Bardocz Peter; (2): Shutterstock.com/hanss; (5) Ausschnitt: Shutterstock.com/Olgastocker; (6): Shutterstock.com/hanss; Ahornblatt: Shutterstock.com/Rawpixel.com; **S. 71** o. v. li. n. re. (1): Shutterstock.com/quietbits; (2): Shutterstock.com/Monkey Business Images; (3): mauritius images/alamy stock photo/NYCPW Photography; (4): Shutterstock.com/RodClementPhotography; (5): Shutterstock.com/f11photo; Mi. li.: Shutterstock.com/GagliardiPhotography; Mi. Mi.: Shutterstock.com/otherstock; Mi. re.: Shutterstock.com/Benedikt Juerges; **S. 74 + S. 75** v. o. li. n. u. re (1): Shutterstock.com/Irina Strelnikova; (2): Shutterstock.com/Trueffelpix; (3): Shutterstock.com/Sudowoodo; (4): Shutterstock.com/robuart; Statistik: Statistics Canada: A Portrait of Canadian Youth, 2019.; **S. 77** v. o. li. n. u. re (1): Shutterstock.com/igor kisselev; (2): Shutterstock.com/grapop; (3): Shutterstock.com/Jon Bilous; (4): Shutterstock.com/Irina Strelnikova; (5): Shutterstock.com/DeiMosz; (6): Shutterstock.com/Maxx-Studio; **S. 81** Mi.: Imago Stock & People GmbH/PA Images/Doug Peters; (1,3 und 7) Ausschnitte: Shutterstock.com/Bardocz Peter; (2): Shutterstock.com/hanss; (5) Ausschnitt: Shutterstock.com/Olgastocker; (6): Shutterstock.com/hanss; Ahornblatt: Shutterstock.com/Rawpixel.com; **S. 83** Männchen in der Karte (Ausschnitt): Shutterstock.com/Bardocz Peter;

Textquellen:

◈ Texte mit diesem Zeichen wurden aus didaktischen Gründen gekürzt oder vereinfacht. Genaue Informationen stehen in diesem Quellenverzeichnis bei den betreffenden Texten.

S. 3 Emma Lazarus: *The new Colossus, aus: Poems and Translations*, Hurd and Houghton, 1867 (◈ Ausschnitt)

S. 24 *Tribal History*: Excerpt from The Mashantucket (Western) Pequot Tribal Nation/ https://www.mptn-nsn.gov/tribalhistory.aspx; Stand: 10.12.2019 (◈ Ausschnitt, gekürzt und leicht verändert)

Liedtexte:

S. 4 Auszug aus: An open letter to NYC. Text: Stephen J. Jr. Bator, Michael Louis Diamond, Adam Keefe Horovitz, John Madansky, Jeff Magnum, Eugene Richard O'Connor, David Lynn Thomas, Adam Nathaniel Yauch, Jimmy Zero. Interpret: Beastie Boys, copyright: Brooklyn Dust Music / Polygram International Publishing Inc / W B Music Corp / Universal Publishing / Neue Welt Musikverlag GmbH